The Social Lives of Networked Students

Rajee Kanagavel

The Social Lives of Networked Students

Mediated Connections

palgrave
macmillan

Rajee Kanagavel
School of Social Sciences
Singapore Management University
Singapore, Singapore

ISBN 978-3-319-96198-9 ISBN 978-3-319-96199-6 (eBook)
https://doi.org/10.1007/978-3-319-96199-6

Library of Congress Control Number: 2018956301

This Palgrave Macmillan imprint is published by the registered company Springer Nature Switzerland AG
The registered company address is: Gewerbestrasse 11, 6330 Cham, Switzerland

Acknowledgements

My experience living in various parts of the world and maintaining transnational relationships (mostly through digital means) is perhaps no surprise given the topic of this book. It has been a great journey, not just working on something I am passionate about, but also sharing the journey with awesome people.

Firstly, I would like to thank my colleague and friend, Andreas Herz. There are some people who instantly and spontaneously extend support and motivate others. He is one of them. It definitely was a great privilege for me to work together with him over the years.

I am not sure whether this book would have been possible without Miranda Lubbers. I will always be grateful for her motivation and enthusiasm, and for sharing her immense knowledge. Her constructive and meticulous feedback was more than just encouragement, which made me work on my PhD with more spirit.

I owe a big thank you to Leonie Dhiman, Hanna Rettig, Elke Kaufmann, Carolin Oppermann, and Gavaza Maluleke, for their guidance, cheerful encouragement, inspiration, deep insights, and fun times during the course of this research project. I will forever remember and cherish the many moments I've spent with each of them, learning from them and pursuing our research together. Thank you for being such a positive influence in my life.

I am grateful to Tabea Noack for being endlessly and characteristically supportive during my time at the University of Hildesheim in Germany. I would also like to extend my gratitude towards the network researchers of Research Network—Network Research (R-N-N-R) for the thought-provoking and enjoyable discussions. I would like to convey my sincere thanks to my web survey developer, Michael Kronenwett, for the survey implementation, and for not losing his patience with the numerous changes I made him go through to achieve the final version of the *IntStudLink* survey.

A special thanks to my friend Yashvanth Chandrasekaran for helping me with the graphics and design. I also really appreciate all of the 287 respondents around the world who took their time to fill in the survey, including their thoughtful comments at the very end.

I dedicate this book to my parents, Maheswari Kanagavel and Kanagavel Natarajan. If it was not for their conviction and faith in my work, I wouldn't have travelled afar on this difficult journey. I take this opportunity to thank my sister Hema Kanagavel who has been nothing but tremendously supportive during different phases of my life. I thank my cousins Shyamala Athiban, Kamal Raj and Adhithya Ganesh for their friendship over the years. I feel incredibly grateful to have such a loving family by my side.

I thank my darling friends: Anna Rahe, Pradeep Kannan, Renu Ramesh, Preethi Prabhakaran, Indhuja Radhakrishnan, Anika Herrmann, Sarina Schade, and Jennifer Bennor. The path was more fun and easy to walk along with you all. I'd like to offer my thanks to my friends Cora Kolossa, Mawusi Beluwada, and Nicola Chasseaud for their most valuable input and feedback during the manuscript preparation phase.

My acknowledgements would be incomplete without my best buddies, Divya Prabha, Shruthi Ingarsal, and Sindhu Sugumar, who put up with me for more than a decade, at the same time helping me through this research. They have been part of my dream from day one and it was they who gave me all of my confidence with the faith that they had in me.

Last but definitely not least, I thank Wolfgang Schröer for supervising my PhD research project which is the foundation of this book. Prof Schröer influentially expressed an adventurous attitude in regard to research. His wit and humility have been an inspiration and always will be. I enjoy working with him and owe him many thanks for everything that he has instilled in me and for all his guidance.

Contents

List of Figures

List of Tables

1

Introduction

At a few minutes past midnight, as soon as he read a message on his mobile phone, Kamal turned on his bedside lamp and walked out through the hallway to fetch his younger sister Adithya. Adithya was already on her way to meet Kamal. They acknowledged the Facebook message they had both received from their cousin-sister Hema and went to the study room where they had a desktop with a good sound system. On the other side of the world, where the sun was shining brightly, Hema replied on the phone, "Sure, it is already on" to her cousin Thileeban who was living in the UK. While I was Skyping in Germany with Thileeban, I Whatsapped my cousin Shyamala, who is living in Bangalore, to join our Skype session. In about ten minutes, I received cross-platform Skype calls from all of my cousins and my sister Hema living in the US, and in less than five minutes we were all part of one Skype video conference call which lasted for another two hours. As complicated as it may sound, it was easy and straightforward to connect ourselves by informing each other about the plan and availability, despite the different time zones and the distance. The connection would have been flawed if there had been any hindrance in the way, be it one person not noticing the message or the technology not liaising exactly at that time. Six of us from four different countries

R. Kanagavel, *The Social Lives of Networked Students*,
https://doi.org/10.1007/978-3-319-96199-6_1

were plugged in, not only because of our availability, but also because our media accessibility helped a lot, in that the chain of connection worked out and the Skype call was accomplished.

As the above anecdote illustrates, connectivity among individuals by using different media (in this case Skype, WhatsApp, and Facebook), gratifying different needs, helps in maintaining contacts and sharing information, no matter where people are living. This increasing ubiquity of digital technologies in everyday life has stimulated discussions about social relationships spanning across borders. This book addresses the intricacies and ambiguities involved in the transformation that communication technologies allegedly bring about across social practices. By engaging the theme of transnational social support against the background of the changing media landscape, I examine its role within the strategies that international students employ in response to experiences of mobility. Of particular interest is the way in which students mobilise social support through transnational links, and the extent to which such links are mediated upon day-to-day activities.

Studies in the field of international migration and international student mobility have acknowledged that moving across national borders impedes the main source of social support, that is, social relationships people maintain with others. Although these discussions seem perennial, the proliferation of new communication technologies that has taken place over the last two decades has radically transformed the functioning of social relationships (Verdery et al. 2018). While it is alleged and empirically shown that geographical proximity and frequent face-to-face contact are no longer necessary conditions for the endurance of social relationships (Hampton and Wellman 2002; Madianou and Miller 2013), there is a paucity of research that focuses on the precise ways in which different media help social relationships carry out their various supportive functions over varying distances in peoples' lives. I have stepped into this void in the literature with this book, discussing the study on international students who are transnationally mobile and digitally active.

In this book, I consider how the social lives of international students are influenced not only by their social relationships such as friends and family, but also by the connections which their social relationships maintain among each other. I precisely focus on transnational social support structures, that is, social practices in relation to the proximity factor and how personal communication media, including in-person contact, help international students deal with these structures in their networks. The transnational social field approach provides acuity in considering social structural practices at both the individual and network level. Although Pries (2007) regards it as nebulous, the field is considered by Mouw et al. (2014) to encompass two components: structure, relating to the intertwined networks, and flow, relating to ideas, remittances, and communication. A heedful examination of the students' support strategies and the extent to which they form support networks and secure social capital across borders provide insights that will raise awareness and inform interventions at an individual, community, and national level.

1.1 Humans Are Social Beings

As members of the human race, we are all to a greater or lesser extent interested in making contact with each other and sharing information and support. We have a concept of our own personal social network, consisting of people with whom we are most susceptible to sharing information, and providing and receiving support. Although in today's world the term "social network" is considered to be synonymous with Facebook and other social media, it is noteworthy that the concept of networking emerged much earlier, before the advent of the internet. It goes back to the notion of the social life of humans in general, which imparts networking irrespective of the media used to stay connected. If social media have to be defined in one word, then it has to be *share*. Is the sharing of information taking place between computer programmes or content passed over to an application? Implicitly this is what is shared, but the communication or sharing takes place between individuals. This book deals with this idea by using a personal network approach to detect networking from the viewpoint of the student.

The connections among individuals build up a social network with ties which are shared and maintained through one or more types of relationship.

The relationships can vary according to the context of meeting, strength, duration, and the type of exchange. The networks divulge how resources flow and disseminate among these individuals, and what kind of structural pattern they exhibit, showing how certain students are more connected than others. The social network analytical approach is a novel concept which advances the field of international student studies, particularly researching transnational social formations and exploring the flow of communication through media channels in their networks. The social network perspective sheds light on the prominence of connections that sustain social processes (Wasserman and Faust 1994; Wellman and Berkowitz 1988). The different types of interaction and exchange that flow through a set of relationships are examined, as well as their effects on the individuals.

1.2 Transnational Social Support

Social support research has gained momentum in recent years. Increased mobility and affordability of transport among the student population has meant that they form and maintain close social relationships from geographically distant areas. Along with increasing research on people's mobility and transnationalism, there has been a redefinition of the connection between personal relationships and community-building processes, and the subject has been placed in relation to forms of social support (Cachia and Jariego 2018; Bojarczuk and Mühlau 2018; Herz 2015). In spite of the still-prevailing notion that "help" necessitates geographical closeness, a different scenario has been emerging in transnational social support research.

Transnational studies have predominantly investigated the relationship between immigrant adaption and assimilation to host countries, and immigrants' transnational practice.[1] There are several studies (Rizvi 2005; Bilecen 2014) employing qualitative and mixed methods which explore the formation of transnational modes of approach among international students. Even though these studies have acknowledged the importance of globalisation processes and communication technologies, little research has been conducted on how personal communication is used. I examine the students' social relationships and the personal communication flow among people in their transnational networks. Although numerous definitions and theories of transnationalism have mentioned the prominence of social relationships inferring the subsistence of social networks, network data is not predominantly used to operationalise the notion (Bilecen et al. 2018). Here, the social network data is used to describe and measure the transnational lives of the international students. In other words, the degree of transnationality is measured by their network connections spanning back to their home countries or somewhere else in the world.

Social support exchange between individuals encompasses instrumental or affective functions ranging from esteem, identity, belonging, companionship, and social reinforcement to socializing (Vaux 1988). In this book I focus on and discuss four different kinds of social support (emotional support, instrumental support, informational support, and social companionship). The interchange of transnational social support takes place at the micro level, that is, between individuals, meaning that the nation states are not pertinent. According to Chambon et al. (2013), "transnational social support is a social process of appropriating and designing social worlds across national borders, in which support activities are performed in either direct or indirect ways". Moreover, new mediators have entered the realm of social ties. Although it can be assumed that social support is unaffected by the medium of relationships, recent research is gradually opening up the question of how different media including face-to-face communication create relationships and develop their own "agency".

1.3 Digital Connectivity

A myriad of developments give rise to a key change in the way individuals interact and in the way each one could interact and keep in contact with others. Unsurprisingly, this has enabled easier access to and communication with people in the network by using high-speed internet availability. It has also afforded the increase of intangible support such as providing information or sharing problems through a medium. Media play a crucial role in the development of migrant communities, as well as how and to which extent its use spans borders and creates transnational connections and identities. These connections are sustained through various elements, with media including in-person contact taking up a bigger portion. Few research studies have focused solely on media use and connectivity among transnational communities. Shumow (2010) shows that the Venezuelan communities in South Florida stay connected to their home country through media. He accomplished this through in-depth qualitative interviews, focusing on the consumption of news and political information about Venezuela through various channels from newspapers to TV, and also how personal communication took place through websites like Facebook.

A network analysis approach has already been applied in studies of the internet, however mostly for different purposes. For example, it is used to study networks of messages cross-posted between selected Usenet newsgroups (Choi and Danowski 2002) and the social networks of students in distance-learning classes (Haythornthwaite 2000). Hlebec et al. (2006) uses a specific network analysis approach to study the internet's impact on the provision of social support, but makes a clear-cut division between internet users and non-internet users. A study of Japanese mothers explores how social support received through the internet affects people's well-being, and how the internet facilitates the provision of social support to friends and neighbours, both online and in "real life" (Miyata 2002). The results show the receipt of social support from weak ties via an online community, and a division is made between real life and online spaces in terms of support provision. In contrast, this book will not differentiate between online and offline social spaces.

Despite the distance-insensitivity of the internet, distance still matters for the overall relationship (Mok et al. 2010), however, different modes of communication have different sensitivities to distance. In this book I propose a media model of eight different types of media: face-to-face contact, letters, text, phone, email, instant messaging (IM), social networking sites, and other video platforms. Until recent times, research on media and distance, or media relating to support, has mainly focused on the internet or media channels such as phone and emails. Boase and

Wellman (2006) examined the frequency with which respondents during that time report keeping in touch with their kin and friends using three different prominent media—face-to-face, telephone, and email. They divided contacts into those living within, or beyond, 50 km, classifying them as nearby and faraway. The results indicate high internet use for greater distance. At the same time, telephone contact remains significant. Compared to relatives, friends were contacted predominately far away, living beyond 50 kms, using email communication. I examine social support entangled with newly emerged media such as social networking sites and IM. The frequency of every media channel use is studied to identify media patterns and then to predict support exchange, strengthening transnational perspectives on social support as well as social network research.

1.4 The Study

The study that emerged from the PhD project referred to in this book aims to find out and explain the social dynamics operating within the international student population, addressing how different media help in maintaining different social support structures through the lens of transnationalism. Drawing data from more than 250 international students from different countries all over the world, I demonstrate this at different levels of analysis: international students' individual practices, their relationships, and the network structure of those relationships. These combinations tend to provide glimpses of the phenomenon of *mediated connections.*

In light of the growing number of noticeable technological developments, it is important to gain an understanding of the experiences of international student mobility in terms of their social lives. The approach of investigating this using social network analysis bridges with concepts within transnational studies. In transnational studies, cross-border interconnections are perceived at the most fundamental level in personal relationships and community-building processes. The network approach is employed, with the international students being the unit of analysis. I focus on the relationships of students whose experience of mobility has

Table 1.1 Characteristics of different network types

	Type I	Type II	Type III	Type IV
	Like or Follow me	*Let's meet asap :)*	*FaceTime or Skype?*	*Where's the party tonight?*
Size	Average	Average	Small	Large
Density	Dense	Dense	Very dense	Sparse
Spatial	Transnational	Local	Household + transnational	Local + transnational
Emotional intensity	Close	Close	Very close	Less close
Mode of contact	Neoteric media	Classic media	Established media	Low media use
Role	Friends/family	Friends/ neighbours	Family/spouse	Friends

the most scope in the participation of their daily lives, irrespective of where they are located.

I explore different types of networks among international students in terms of network structure, average closeness, geographical dimensions, and media use (see Table 1.1). I identify four patterns: "*Like or Follow me*" (transnational networks with extensive use of social media), "*Let's meet asap :)*" (local networks where face-to-face contact is the most prevalent), "*Facetime or Skype*" (small, dense networks of strong ties where email and Skype are often used), and "*Where's the party tonight?*" (large, sparse networks of weaker ties with low media use). I examine numerous aspects of the international students' networks and also demonstrate how these networks influence the exchange of social support. Moreover, I examine when and how support multiplexity, that is, exchange of more than one type of support, is received or given. Both the structural and relational aspects of the networks are considered when studying this phenomenon. In short, *The Social Lives of Networked Students* examines the social networks of international students, exploring the ways in which they experience social support and use different media, including face-to-face contact, over shorter and longer distances.

The central argument of the book is that co-presence is not a prerequisite for support exchange. The aspect of transnationality is matched with an analysis of connectivity without the assumption that co-present support is superior, or at least with an open mind to the way virtual forms of support are transforming ways of providing support and being co-present. I argue that the best approach is not either/or, but rather asking how the use of communication technologies is transforming the way we care (even in proximate settings) and our ability to receive or give support across distance. I consider face-to-face contact as one of the media tools used for communication for support exchange. Different media use (including physical presence) influences the decision as to when and how support is transferred across distance. This habitat embraces the expansion rather than truncation of networks, confirming the importance of circulation using network approach in addition to the traditional dyadic phenomenon, that is, looking at the relationship level.

Although the central argument of the book is framed around co-presence and geographical distance, I discuss all four forms of social support of the study throughout the book—emotional support, instrumental support, informational support, and social companionship. The media usage patterns in the international students' networks in terms of network typologies are examined by relating them to each type of support, thus providing a better understanding of support exchange. Moreover, the book will look at multiplex support, that is, two or more support dimensions exchanged with the same tie. For example, a friend living in the same neighbourhood can help with an economics assignment and at the same time provide advice on personal matters, that is, provide both instrumental support and emotional support. In the study, it is found that co-presence is necessary for the exchange of multistranded social support. This in turn proposes that the transnational support is single-stranded and that transnational ties serve a unique purpose. Media use alters the necessity of co-presence for multiplex support provision.

Although the group of international students provides an adequate context to analyse support exchanges in transnational contexts, I examine networks of expatriates, that is, professionals in continuous and itinerant international mobility, by using a short survey to incorporate a comparative reference when it comes to mobility. In this way, I reflect on the aspect of mobility in the structure of networks and in support exchanges taking place in both expatriates' and international students' networks.

Concerning student mobility and the conforming communicative practices, the results of the study indicate that support tied to physical co-presence in the past has the potential to be mobile now through new communication technologies. The four different network types offer a perspective on the variation of media use and on transnational social formations despite the distance. In terms of support received as well as given, a crucial factor is network size, that is, the number of people in the network and tie strength. Although the internet is integrated into students' transnational lives, the syntheses of new and traditional media, including face-to-face communication, act as modes of interaction for support exchange leading to 'digital' social transformation in the lives of students.

1.5 The Field

International students are stimulated to adjust to their new academic, social, and cultural environment as quickly as possible, and usually they do. The formal procedures of visa processing and registration at the university allow completion of an academic programme within the allotted time period. These two developments, one of adjustment to the new culture and one of maintaining the original one, are not mutually exclusive, and frequently run parallel to one another. The concept of transnationalism as a process through which people adjust to a new culture but maintain social and cultural ties to their home countries (Schiller et al. 1995), helps us to understand the subtle position in which students locate themselves. When students come to live and study in the host country for a few years, the question is not if their networks change, but to what degree. On their arrival, students face a variety of challenges that make everyday life complicated, coping with different things such as food, weather, and transportation. It takes a while to cope and also integrate into the new society with the establishment of social connections and participation in social life.

A sample of 287 international students from different countries is considered in the study. A self-administrated online survey (called *IntStudLink*) is used to reach the students who are widespread across different countries. One of the interesting characteristics of the personal networks of international students is their geographical spread. Coming to the geographical distribution of the survey, Fig. 1.1 shows the vast dispersion of the survey in European countries and North America.

Fig. 1.1 Geographical distribution of the survey

The other survey participants are scattered over different parts of the world, from Los Angeles to Auckland, which speaks for the success of the snowball sampling process employed in the data collection process. In the following section, I will describe the various characteristics of the international students.

Personal Characteristics

There has been a tremendous increase in the number of students enrolled abroad for studies outside their home countries or country of citizenship. With an estimated nearly five million[2] international students in tertiary education[3] all around the world, the globalisation and growth of the education system is demonstrated, with a chain evolving around the sending as well as host countries. In this section, the characteristics of the sample will be compared to the characteristics described in the Organisation for Economic Co-operation and Development (OECD) international student study on student mobility published by the UNESCO Institute for Statistics (UIS).[4] The sample will be compared to the OECD data on international[5] students. Although there are a minimal number of biases, several characteristics show a similar pattern such that the comparability is rational when describing the target population.

The education indicators from the OECD study along with the *IntStudLink* survey results are summarised for comparison in Table 1.2. Starting with the personal characteristics, national and geographical diversity are examined. The data from both the survey and OECD study were refined to match the criteria. The categorisation of countries by vari-

Table 1.2 Comparison of distribution of international students by region of birth (1 = *IntStudLink*, 2 = OECD)

	Africa		Americas		Asia		Europe		Oceania	
Origin	1	2	1	2	1	2	1	2	1	2
Africa	13.1	–	0	5.7	0	–	2.5	6.8	0.4	1.9
Americas	1.3	–	1.3	19.7	0	–	8.5	8.4	0	4.1
Asia	2.1	–	9.3	42.2	1.7	–	19.1	14.3	2.1	74.3
Europe	2.1	–	2.1	25.6	2.1	–	29.2	57.8	1.3	5.8
Oceania	0	–	0.4	0.6	0	–	1.3	0.2	0	5.7

ous continents and regions follows the United Nations composition of geographical regions. The major five geographical regions, that is, Africa, the Americas, Asia, Europe, and Oceania, are further segregated into various countries.[6]

The global flow of international students depends on various factors, starting from economic policies drawn for every country at the macro level to personal choice at the micro level. Countries where English is spoken predominantly have a record of receiving more students than other countries. The most popular destination remains North America, and Asian students are the highest numbers, accounting for 53 per cent of all students studying abroad in 2013, according to the OECD. In the *IntStudLink* survey data, the countries where the respondents lived and also filled in the survey was not as widely spread as the countries of origin to which they belonged. The geographical distribution of the respondents by country of residence (n = 287) is as follows: 83 respondents from Germany (forming the majority of nearly 29 per cent); 60 from South Africa (21 per cent)[7]; and 31 from the United States (nearly 11 per cent). Following these three main destinations, many international students are attracted to Western European countries like the Netherlands (6 per cent), the United Kingdom (4.2 per cent), Belgium (3.2 per cent), and France (2.8 per cent), as well as to the Scandinavian countries Finland (2.8 per cent), Denmark (2.1 per cent), and Sweden (4.2 per cent). Apart from this, it is noteworthy to mention Australia, which serves as a destination for nine respondents. The majority of the other students are studying in other European countries.[8] As there are many countries to be represented in a graph, the countries of residence of the international students are illustrated in Fig. 1.2 according to the main five geographical regions.[9]

Considering the main regions, Europe has the highest number of respondents to the survey. This occurrence may be due to the snowball sampling where the survey was forwarded through connections, and particularly Germany ranking first reflects this reach. Countries may vary in their international students' intake, be it in terms of academic excellence, visa regulations, or tuition fee structures. Apart from the sampling, it can be rightly assumed that these factors most likely put a few countries on a higher pedestal than others. In that regard, Europe even has policies pertaining to education to foster student mobility.

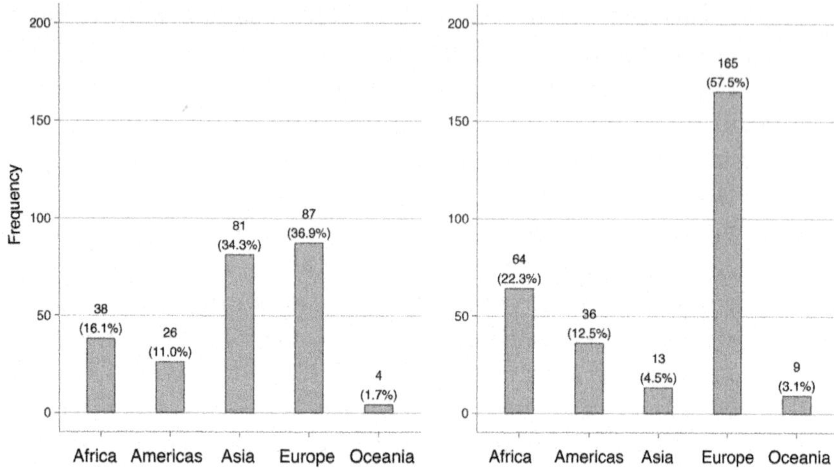

Fig. 1.2 The left-hand figure shows the frequency of distribution of the international students' region-wise countries of birth (*N* = 236) and the right-side figure shows the distribution of international students' region-wise countries of residence (*N* = 287), both according to the five geographical regions

Coming to the countries of origin, the majority of the respondents were Germans (12.6 per cent), Indians (14.2 per cent), Chinese (5.2 per cent), and Americans (4 per cent). Europe ranks first even in terms of birth, as Europeans tend to be mobile and to enrol in a country abroad for studies. Looking at the distribution of the countries of birth[10] in Fig. 1.2, it is apparent that there is almost the same number of people in the sample who were born in Asia as there were in Europe. The profile of international students in terms of their origin is quite pervasive, covering all the regions. The proportion of Asian students enrolled in other countries for studies comprises mostly Indians and Chinese in the survey, while European students are mainly German and Spanish.

The regions of Europe, Africa, and North America tend to be the most favoured destinations among the respondents in the sample, while a clear distinction is made between countries. Although it is not unforeseen for Europe and North America to host many international students, the trend in Southern Africa is unprecedented. This eccentricity might be conventional but not reported widely. As the definition of international students goes, cross-bordering takes place within a specific region as well as between two regions across oceans. According to UNESCO statistics, around three quarters of the international student population within EU countries come from another EU country. This reflects the effect of mobility policies established in these countries. In Table 1.2[11] the survey data is compared to the OECD according to the regions of destination and origin, to take heed of the population in general. Examining the two groups' data reveals that there is a similarity in the case of Europe in terms of studying in the same region as the region of birth. There is a bias towards Africans studying in their region in the *IntStudLink* survey. The proportions of both Asians and Americans studying in Europe coincide in both samples.

While mobility is characterised in numerous ways, be it intra- or international mobility, it was found that there were nearly equal proportions of intra- and intercontinental mobility. Nearly 46 per cent of the students moved from their home countries to their countries of residence inside the same continent, and the remaining students (i.e. 54 per cent) moved between different continents, counted as trans-Atlantic or trans-Pacific mobility. Europeans were in the majority, representing around 84 per cent of the mobility which took place in the same continent. Apart from them, Africans accounted for 14 per cent of intra-continental mobility.

The *IntStudLink* survey sample is biased in terms of gender. While nearly 51 per cent of the OECD population is female, nearly 67 per cent of the respondents in the sample are female. This might also be due to the conventional belief that surveys are filled in more often by females and older people. The proportion of female survey participants is higher than the proportion of male respondents. This is similar to studies (Bilecen 2014; Herz 2015) where the data was collected using surveys. Out of the 287 respondents, information on relationship status was recorded for 236, or nearly 80 per cent, of the respondents. Respondents who are in a relationship (36.9 per cent) and married (8.4 per cent) at the time of the survey account for nearly half of the respondents. It can be rightly said that nearly half of the respondents are therefore either in a relationship, married or together by common law (see Table 1.3).

The mean age of the respondents is 25.6 years (SD = 4.7 years) with a minimum of 19 and a maximum of 43. The average international student in the sample was born in 1988. Of the 241 respondents who answered

Table 1.3 Personal and socio-economic characteristics

	n	Per cent
Gender (*N* = 241)		
Male	83	34.4
Female	158	65.6
Relationship status (*N* = 236)		
Single	107	37.3
In a relationship	106	36.9
Married	20	7
Common-law/widowed	3	1
Education (*N* = 240)		
Bachelors	70	29.2
Masters	92	38.3
PhD/doctoral	57	23.8
Exchange/guest	13	5.4
Other	8	3.3
Residential status (*N* = 287)		
Student permit	204	71.1
Residence permit for researchers	11	3.8
Family residence permit	2	0.7
Permanent (settlement) residence permit	20	7
Work permit	11	3.8
Citizenship of the residing country	9	3.1
I don't know	10	3.5
Others	20	7
Mode of fee payment (*N* = 287)		
My family pays	112	39
My own savings	58	20.2
Part-time job	41	14.3
Loan from a financial institution	19	6.6
Salaried position at the university	28	9.8
Scholarship/grant/fellowship	108	37.6
Other	14	4.9

this question (who also completed the survey), 56.4 per cent fall into the 22–27 year old age category. Age is skewed towards the right, manifesting a positive skew towards the youngest of the respondents.

Most of the respondents have been in the host country for a year or less than a year. Around 30 per cent of the students (84 out of 287 respondents) arrived in their current country of residence in the same year as the survey was conducted, while another 30 per cent arrived in the previous year, 2012, and 38 respondents arrived in 2011. Another 80 respondents arrived before the year 2011. So, it can be rightly said that most of them have been in their current country of residence for less than 3 years. The median year is 1 and the mean of the number of years in the country is 2.06 years (SD = 0.15). Duration is positively skewed, and the predominance of the population arrived in the host country within six years before the survey.

Socio-Economic Characteristics

As the OECD (2011) proposed, global mobility is assuaged by inter- and intra-regional migration patterns of students to a substantial extent. It is essential to view the paradigm from the viewpoint of the socio-economic characteristics of the international students. The flow within selected regions, such as in Europe or Oceania, tends to demonstrate the development of geopolitical areas, such as ties between Asia-Pacific countries and among European countries beyond the EU (Altbach et al. 2009).

To view the educational status in the survey, the highest educational attainment was captured. There are distinctions in the level of tertiary education according to the type of programme and number of years of enrolment. The three main categories as put forth by the OECD are tertiary A, tertiary B, and advanced research programmes. While tertiary A comprises full-time normal programmes, tertiary B consists mainly of short and vocational programmes. Bachelor's and master's programmes fall under the category of tertiary A, and there is a predominance of this category in the survey data. Of the 240 respondents who provided information on their highest level of education, over 162 students are doing either their master's (38.3 per cent) or bachelor's (29.2 per cent). This coincides with the OECD figure of 78.4 per cent of students enrolled in tertiary A programmes.

There is no large difference in the sample between the number of students enrolled in bachelor's and PhD/doctoral programmes (23.8 per cent). This is interesting, as the courses are a minimum of three years and usually protracted. This is in contrast to the notion of international students mostly being in the host country for a short period. It also indicates that there is a recent increase in the number of international students enrolling in full-time courses which last a minimum of three years.

Information on whether the students are degree-mobile[12] or credit-mobile[13] (King et al. 2010) is not addressed in the survey. But this is compensated for by the information on duration of the time since arrival and the type of programme enrolled in, in the current country of residence. There are many exchange programmes in the EU, like the Erasmus programme, which facilitate mobility, and a semester abroad is imperative in some universities. In India, for example, although it is atypical to go abroad while pursuing a course in general, students are more likely to go abroad for a master's programme after gaining a degree. It is noticed that only five per cent are exchange students, who are pursuing a semester abroad while being enrolled as master's or bachelor's students in their home country or another country, and came to the current country as a guest/international student for a relatively short time—thus imparting information that most of the respondents are credit-mobile. Although the time period of the master's programme is longer than that of exchange programmes, it is still short. However, the data reveals the importance of being abroad even for that time span, especially for specialisation in particular subjects and gaining more expertise in one particular area during a master's programme.

Coming to the field of education, there is predominance among students studying engineering in the *IntStudLink* survey, whereas the categories of social sciences, business, and law had a large number of students in the OECD data. Although there is a difference here, the majority of different fields of education in OECD data coincide with the survey data. The data shows that one tenth of the respondents (10.3 per cent) study engineering, followed by business (9.1 per cent), law (7.8 per cent), and sociology (6.2 per cent). As most of the respondents are studying professional courses like engineering or business, it is discernible that the students are aspiring to be upwardly mobile. This could also result in full-time enrolment rather than a transient stay, to get a good résumé out of their travel experiences.

Regarding economic and social policies, visa regulations can implicitly or explicitly—depending on the region and country—pave the way for mobility as well. The student status in the residing country is documented to evaluate the situation, that is, whether the student has a student, residence, or work permit for the country of residence. Approximately three quarters of the respondents (71.1 per cent) possess a student permit visa indicative of a temporary stay in the country of residence. Doctoral students who are pursuing research hold resident permits enabling researchers in many countries to stay for relatively longer than with other study programmes. Permanent residents account for seven per cent, which points to the fact that they might settle, or have made some concrete plans, in the country of residence. The major responses show a huge difference, as the latter percentage is much lower than the higher percentage of respondents living with a student permit. This contributes to the fact that the international students live in their current country of residence for a short span, but the consequences of this short stay could be very different at a later stage.

Approximately 60 per cent of the students are studying with financial help from the family or on their own expenses, suggesting that the student's choice of country is dependent on the economic conditions of the student and their family. At the same time, the nearly 40 per cent of respondents getting scholarships and grant availability indicates the economic milieu at a macro level. Moreover, lower tuition fees could also be the grounds for choosing a particular programme or country. For example, countries like the US impose high tuition fees, whereas Germany and France have the same tuition fees for both regular (German students/citizens of the country) and international students, which is a reason why students flock to these countries.

University Settings

The social life of a person largely depends on the place or type of surroundings where they are positioned. To determine the setting, information on the size of the university (in terms of its students) and the size of the city (in terms of its inhabitants) was collected. Nearly half of the respondents (108 out of 236) study at a university where there are more than 10,000 but less than 50,000 students. While 30 per cent live in a metropolitan city which has more than 500,000 inhabitants, nearly half of the respondents live in a city with fewer than 500,000 inhabitants, and one fifth live in a town with fewer than 100,000 inhabitants. The size of the city plays a vital role in commuting to different places within the same city to meet people and maintain local ties in their social network.

In order to get an idea of the social life of the international students and to study the integration with other students in the local as well as university settings, participation in activities in and out of university as well as their language skills were evaluated. Over half of the students (52.6 per cent) are members of some type of organisation. Students are involved in activities with people from the same origin (37.5 per cent) and with mostly other international students (44.7 per cent). An acquaintance of mine from Korea met most of her friends at the local church organisation where she is part of the choir and weekend service. She eventually met her boyfriend there, who is also Korean. At times, language acts as a deciding factor for choosing a country to go to. Apparently, the more fluent international students are in English, the more probable it is that they will have a smoother changeover into the new environment (Poyrazli 2003), but the scenario can be different when English is not spoken as the first language. In the study, equal numbers of students are unaware (34.5 per cent) as well as knowledgeable (34.9 per cent) about the local language spoken in the current country of residence.

1.6 Organisation of This Book

Chapter 2 introduces a theoretical framework that interconnects the concepts of personal networks, transnationalism, and social support. I elucidate how the relationships in the networks of students influence the mechanisms of social support and transnationalism, rather than their mere activities and resources accounting for both. I discuss certain important attributes of network members such as geographical proximity and support exchange.

In Chap. 3, I discuss the use of media and its repercussions on international students' relationships and support, and whether it leads to social transformation. Rather than discussing a need to recognise that quality social interaction exists in the offline realm more than online, the book focuses on social processes in the context of technological mediation in support exchanges. I argue that even face-to-face contact is mediated, in a way, when it comes to personal communication. The main question of whether co-presence is necessary for support exchange is thoroughly discussed. Although the categories of media are broadly classified, the frequency and the type can add more substance to the networks. The chapter ends with the introduction of three profiles of media use: *Classic media, Neoteric media and Established media.*

In Chap. 4, I describe the structural (such as network size and interconnectedness of the members who make up the network) and compositional properties (such as tie strength, duration, and family) of the international students' networks. As transnationalism is operationalised in this study through the geographical dispersion of respondents' social networks, I explain transnationality at the level of both the individual and the network.

Chapter 5 addresses the media patterns observed among the international students. Four different patterns of networks were found by combining profiles of media use along with the structural and compositional network characteristics: Type I (*Like or Follow me*), Type II (*Let's meet asap :)*), Type III (*FaceTime or Skype?*) and Type IV (*Where's the party tonight?*). Each network exhibited a different pattern of relationships and media used for maintaining contact. To illustrate the clusters, I describe specific cases of international students belonging to each cluster in the study.

Chapter 6 focuses on the determinants of social support exchange, considering frequency of media use and other characteristics of international students. I begin the chapter by discussing the network effect and the flow of information, including social support, through different media patterns. The final part of the chapter addresses support multiplexity, which is an important feature of a tie. Multiplexity denotes the degree to which two or more kinds of ties concur between the international students and their network members (who are elicited using the network survey questions). As the elicitation of the personal network members happens through the social support questions employed, the relationships are already multiplexed when other contents of the relationship are measured for multiplexity. The provision of different kinds of support will help in understanding multiplexity, which is the overlapping of support dimensions. As I sample supportive ties through the survey, I will analyse whether ties give specialised (uniplex) versus multistranded (multiplex) support. The relative prominence of relational and structural effects on the provision of social support will be identified through multilevel analysis.

In Chap. 7, I reflect on the results, and discuss strengths and limitations of the study. I review the implications of the findings along with future directions for research. I compare the students' networks with expatriates' networks and discuss the abstraction of mobility. The accessibility of these new technologies is not just transforming distant relationships but is affecting proximate ones during support practices and experiences. I conclude by discussing how the degree of connectedness in today's digital age can be contextualised with social transformation.

Notes

1. Transnational practices could be actions or behaviours of individuals, such as sending remittances or receiving fee money, travelling back and forth, or even making local friendships.
2. Source: Organisation of Economic Co-operation and Development (OECD) http://www.oecd.org/statistics/ July 2016.
3. According to the World Bank, tertiary education in general indicates all post-secondary education in institutions, including colleges, technical training institutes, community colleges, nursing schools, research laboratories, centres of excellence, and distance learning centres.
4. http://data.uis.unesco.org Data Source: UIS database, OECD, Eurostat Published: May 2017.
5. According to the UNESCO Institute for Statistics, the OECD and Eurostat, international students are defined as students who are not residents of their country of study, or those who received their prior education in another country. Although OECD reports produced results on both international students and foreign students, international students'

data will be the primary focus here. Unlike international students, foreign students are long-term residents or born in the country of study, but do not hold citizenship of that country.

6. http://unstats.un.org/unsd/methods/m49/m49regin.htm \\ Geographical region and composition: Africa (Eastern Africa, Middle Africa, Northern Africa, Southern Africa, Western Africa), Americas (Latin America and the Caribbean, Central America, South America), North America, Asia (Central Asia, Eastern Asia, Southern Asia, South-Eastern Asia, Western Asia), Europe (Eastern Europe, Northern Europe, Southern Europe, Western Europe), Oceania (Australia and New Zealand, Melanesia, Micronesia, Polynesia).
7. The percentage in brackets corresponds to the percentage of international students enrolled in that country.
8. The distribution of the rest of the countries of residence is as follows: five from Turkey (2), four from Canada (1.6), four from Spain (1.6), three from Israel (1.2), two from Ireland (0.8) and Luxembourg (0.8), and one respondent from each of Albania, Andorra, Botswana, Bulgaria, Malaysia, Italy, Lesotho, Madagascar, Nigeria, Norway, Pakistan, Philippines, Singapore, Cambodia, Swaziland, and Switzerland.
9. The absolute value of the respondents in each geographical region is as follows:

   Africa (65): Southern Africa (Swaziland, South Africa, Lesotho) 62; Eastern Africa (Mozambique) 1; Middle Africa (Nigeria, Angola) 2;
   Americas (38): North America (United States, Canada) 38;
   Asia (13): Southern Asia (India) 1; Western Asia (Turkey, Israel) 6; Southeastern Asia (Singapore, Malaysia, Cambodia) 6;
   Europe (160): Northern Europe (United Kingdom, Sweden, Norway, Denmark, Finland, Ireland) 41; Southern Europe (Spain, Italy, Albania) 5; Western Europe (Switzerland, Netherlands, Luxembourg, France, Belgium, Germany) 119; Eastern Europe (Russia) 1;
   Oceania (9): Australia 9.

10. The absolute value of the frequency distribution of the students' countries of birth are as follows:

    Africa (41)—Northern Africa (2) Tunisia 1, Morocco 1 | Southern Africa (11) Botswana 1, Swaziland 3, South Africa 1, Lesotho 4, Namibia 2 | Eastern Africa (7) Ethiopia 1, Kenya 4, Sudan 1, Mauritius

1, Madagascar 1 | Middle Africa (21) Zimbabwe 12, Zambia 1, Congo 2, Cameroon 1, Nigeria 4, Angola 1
Americas (27)—Northern America (14) United States 9, Canada 5 | South America (9) Peru 1, Colombia 4, Chile 2, Brazil 2 | Central America (2) Mexico 1, Costa Rica 1 | Caribbean (2) Puerto Rico 1, Jamaica 1
Asia (82)—Southern Asia (39) Bangladesh 1, India 34, Iran 1, Pakistan 3 | Western Asia (9) Azerbaijan 1, Lebanon 1, Turkey 7 | Eastern Asia (20) Taiwan 2, South Korea 4, Japan 1, China 13 | South-Eastern Asia (13) Vietnam 2, Cambodia 1, Thailand 2, Singapore 2, Indonesia 2, Malaysia 1, Philippines 2, Burma 1 | Central Asia (1) Kazakhstan 1
Europe (86)—Northern Europe (10) United Kingdom 5, Finland 1, Iceland 1, Lithuania 3 | Southern Europe (18) Andorra 2, Spain 7, Greece 1, Slovenia 1, Serbia 1, Italy 4, Albania 2 | Western Europe (39) Switzerland 1, Netherlands 2, France 5, Germany 31 | Eastern Europe (19) Ukraine 2, Slovakia 1, Romania 1, Poland 6, Moldova 1, Hungary 2, Bulgaria 2, Russia 5
Oceania (4)—Australia and New Zealand (4) Australia 4.

11. Notes: (1) International students enrolled from a given region of origin as a percentage of all international students in the region of destination. Each region comprises countries segregated in terms of United Nations composition of countries.

    (2) Both the regions in the OECD data cover only OECD countries in terms of origin and destination, except for Japan. The percentage of the countries, region-wise, was calculated to match the *IntStudLink* data. This is the reason for the absence of data under Africa and Asia columns.

    (3) Year of reference for OECD data is 2011 and the *IntStudLink* survey was conducted in 2013.

    (4) The total of the *IntStudLink* respondents in terms of the regions of birth will be 100, whereas OECD will not be equal to 100 as the category of people who had missing values in the OECD is not reported here.
12. Within-programme mobility, which is enrolment in another university for a brief period of time as part of the current programme, for example Erasmus.
13. Whole-programme mobility where the student moves abroad for an entire programme.

References

Altbach, P. G., Reisberg, L., & Rumbley, L. (2009). *Trends in global higher education: Tracking an academic revolution: A report prepared for the UNESCO 2009 world conference on higher education*. UNESCO.

Bilecen, B. (2014). *International student mobility and transnational friendships*. Palgrave Macmillan.

Bilecen, B., Gamper, M., & Lubbers, M. J. (2018). The missing link: Social network analysis in migration and transnationalism. *Social Networks, 53*, 1–3.

Boase, J., & Wellman, B. (2006). Personal relationships: On and off the Internet. In A. L. Vangelisti & D. Perlman (Eds.), *The Cambridge handbook of personal relationships* (Vol. 8, pp. 709–723). Cambridge: Cambridge University Press.

Bojarczuk, S., & Mühlau, P. (2018). Mobilising social network support for childcare: The case of Polish migrant mothers in Dublin. *Social Networks, 53*, 101–110.

Cachia, R., & Jariego, I. M. (2018). Mobility types, transnational ties and personal networks in four highly skilled immigrant communities in Seville (Spain). *Social Networks, 53*, 111–124.

Chambon, A., Schröer, W., & Schweppe, C. (Eds.). (2013). *Transnational social support* (Vol. 7). Routledge.

Choi, J. H., & Danowski, J. A. (2002). Making a global community on the net – Global village or global metropolis?: A Network analysis of usenet newsgroups. *Journal of Computer-Mediated Communication, 7*(3), JCMC735.

Hampton, K., & Wellman, B. (2002). The not so global village of Netville. In B. Wellman & C. Haythornthwaite (Eds.), *The Internet in everyday life* (pp. 345–371). Oxford, UK: Blackwell.

Haythornthwaite, C. (2000). Online personal networks: Size, composition and media use among distance learners. *New Media & Society, 2*(2), 195–226.

Herz, A. (2015). Relational constitution of social support in migrants' transnational personal communities. *Social Networks, 40*, 64–74.

Hlebec, V., Manfreda, K. L., & Vehovar, V. (2006). The social support networks of internet users. *New Media & Society, 8*(1), 9–32.

King, R., Findlay, A., & Ahrens, J. (2010). International student mobility literature review.

Madianou, M., & Miller, D. (2013). *Migration and new media: Transnational families and polymedia*. Routledge.

Miyata, K. (2002). Social support for Japanese mothers online and offline. In B. Wellman & C. Haythornthwaite (Eds.), *The internet in everyday life* (pp. 520–548). Oxford, UK: Blackwell.
Mok, D., Wellman, B., & Carrasco, J. (2010). Does distance matter in the age of the internet? *Urban Studies, 47*(13), 2747–2783.
Mouw, T., Chavez, S., Edelblute, H., & Verdery, A. (2014). Binational social networks and assimilation: A test of the importance of transnationalism. *Social Problems, 61*(3), 329–359.
Poyrazli, S. (2003). Ethnic identity and psychosocial adjustment among international students. *Psychological Reports, 92*(2), 512–514.
Pries, L. (2007). Transnationalism: Trendy catch-all or specific research programme? A proposal for transnational organisation studies as a micro-macro-link.
Programme for International Student Assessment. (2011). PISA 2009 at a Glance. OECD Publishing.
Rizvi, F. (2005). International education and the production of cosmopolitan identities. In *Transnational Seminar Series*.
Schiller, N. G., Basch, L., & Blanc, C. S. (1995). From immigrant to transmigrant: Theorizing transnational migration. *Anthropological Quarterly, 68*, 48–63.
Shumow, M. (2010). A foot in both worlds: Transnationalism and media use among Venezuelan immigrants in South Florida. *International Journal of Communication, 4*, 21.
Vaux, A. (1988). *Social support: Theory, research, and intervention*. Praeger Publishers.
Verdery, A. M., Mouw, T., Edelblute, H., & Chavez, S. (2018). Communication flows and the durability of a transnational social field. *Social Networks, 53*, 57–71.
Wasserman, S., & Faust, K. (1994). *Social network analysis: Methods and applications* (Vol. 8). Cambridge University Press.
Wellman, B., & Berkowitz, S. D. (Eds.). (1988). *Social structures: A network approach* (Vol. 2). CUP Archive.

2

From a Network Theory to a Social Phenomenon

It could be chance meetings or just destined by birth. Whatever it may be, each relationship is of its own kind. Although some life-changing connections might have been missed by being idle and solitary, there are new relationships waiting to be made every now and then. What if I had not been allotted to that section in my class? What if that one message on Facebook had gone unseen? What if I hadn't registered for a tandem partner? When a relationship is initiated and dealt with in a particular way for a particular purpose, it is nurtured and developed accordingly from that stage into something which develops into a relationship with someone who belongs to our own social network.

Proximity plays a role in the development process of social relationships. The core of an international student's social life starts with, and revolves around, the university. In that case, campus connectors as well as good transportation systems in terms of commuting contribute to social life. This applies to other parts of the town when it comes to socialising and meeting up with friends in the city. Social sphere extends from places within the limits of the city to places that are continents away, depending on the location of the members in the networks. Distance clearly plays a role when it comes to exchanging support resources in daily life. This is where the intersection of media comes in.

R. Kanagavel, *The Social Lives of Networked Students*,
https://doi.org/10.1007/978-3-319-96199-6_2

There has been a growing focus on the role of social networks and social support in connecting the concept of transnationalism. I will elaborate on each of the theoretical concepts in more detail in this chapter. Research on networks and communication media, which will form the rest of the theoretical context for the study, will be explained in the next chapter. This framework contributes to the knowledge of social networking as social support by focusing on relations and processes of social support occurring cross-nationally. By providing a distinct focus on transnational forms of engaging support resources, the findings discussed in the book will lead to a significant new understanding of the various methods employed by international students, including the use of media as a connecting tool. Looking at social support from this perspective is well-suited to the analysis of social support in cross-national contexts and emphasises the complex ways through which students can interpret the availability of support.

2.1 The "I, Me, Myself" Approach

The essence of social networks in one's life epitomises establishing long-lasting social relationships as well as everyday interactions. To network in recent times, regardless of where a person resides, alludes to engaging with different media used to maintain relationships. This is not necessarily for maintaining contact with those living abroad or far away, but to connect with people in the everyday life context. This in turn helps in sharing time with other people, which leads to giving or receiving social support. The difference in the usage of media tools and the flow of resources in these networks in different places can arise because of transnational practices, which are potential features in one's everyday life.

As the relationships emanate from one particular individual in that individual's network, they are subjective and differ from one person to another. Although strategies and external factors can lead to indistinguishable patterns in different networks as such, an individual will be at the helm when it comes to defining relationships in their very own network. The idiosyncratic nature of an individual's network has led researchers to name these networks "egocentric networks". As the name implies, egocentric networks are focused and centred around a particular individual (who is the ego), including its embeddedness. Although the terms "egocentric networks" and "personal networks" are used interchangeably in the literature, research claims that personal networks are egocentric networks within the whole network of the world (McCarty et al. 2011). While egocentric networks are networks around an *ego* that are extracted from complete networks, personal networks are generated from the viewpoint of an *ego* using survey and interview instruments.

Personal network studies usually target the intrinsically social quality of what is happening inside a network and look for community only in spatially defined areas. Conventionally, this typically means interviewing a slice or a huge portion of the individual's network. In this way, the contents of the network are studied through its composition and relational patterns. In other words, personal network data encompasses data about the *ego* and data about individuals known as *alters* who share certain ties—a network term for relationships—with the ego (Hanneman and Riddle 2011). A relationship shared with the ego can belong to people from different social spheres, from the sense of belonging attained at birth, or even in various settings like a school or neighborhood.

A distinction is made in the literature between personal networks and personal communities by claiming that a personal network encompasses thousands of weak ties, as in Facebook, whereas the personal community focuses on the relationships shared in our daily lives, consisting mainly of family and friends (Hogan 2009; McEwen 2010). This reflects the definition of personal community consisting of meaningful relationships that a person belongs to, instead of considering communities as confined to institutions such as neighbourhood, family, or organisations. The students' networks elicited in the study are mostly close, and so can be referred to as personal communities.

According to Barry Wellman (2011), there are three forms of networked communities: little boxes, glocalisation, and networked individualism. While little boxes refer to closely packed networks connecting individuals door-to-door, glocalised networks are sparse, with clusters connecting individuals locally and globally. Networked individualism has proliferated in the past decade with the advent of cutting-edge and ground-breaking innovative technologies. No matter where one travels or moves, social relationships follow the individual. This concept can be brought in line with the theoretical framework of transnationalism I follow in this book. The degree to which social networks and everyday activities have in fact surpassed the geographical boundaries of the nation-state affects how individual social relations and networks are affected by the new arrangement of boundaries, space, and distance. Terms like "seamless world" and "borderless" entail the new type of interdependence that structures have developed, which is in contrast to the obsolete idea of national containers (Mau 2010). They can no longer impose barriers on the extensions of relationships and there can be no control of the flow of information with the proliferation of these advancements.

Network studies are intricate in their own way in terms of considering individuals as the unit of analysis and keeping track of several different types of information (Campbell and Lee 1991). A common interest can be shared in a network; for example, one might add a person to one's Facebook network for the purpose of perpetual communication or to engage in an activity of shared interest. These social connections form a matrix with the structural dimensions serving a function or controlling the flow of information. Information flow could be taking place between the ego and an alter, from two alters interconnected by another means, or from individual or unrelated alters. All things being equal, the matrix is based upon social support structures where the ego decides with whom to connect with the objective question of who will provide support.

Research on social support emerged from the field of health, shifting the focus to community networks, the supportive resources that community ties convey, and their consequences for mental and physical well-being and longevity (Fischer 1984; Wellman 1992). Social support as such is confounded with other network-based but distinct social factors such as integration and cohesion. The content of the ties—social support—is the degree to which a person's basic social needs are gratified through interaction with others (Thoits 1982). These interactions, which influence the support taking place transcending borders, constitute the crux of the examination.

Numerous studies have shown that social relationships help people to improve their lives by providing memories, intimate support, and valuable information. Nevertheless, one shortcoming of having these relationships is that contacting them often requires substantial time and energy. Taking this into consideration, the greatest accomplishment for a person as such could be keeping in touch with people in their network, be it friends or family, no matter whether they are far or near. Rather than relying only on routine interactions with people in the local environment, people have meaningful and close relationships with people spanning all over the world by using their preferred media following their own networking strategies.

The relationships, and the relationships intertwined within people in the network, make up the personal network data. Personal network data have a multilevel structure: network composition, which consists of the aggregated characteristics of the network members (alters) and ties (ego-alter relations) in each network (for example, the mean frequency of contact that the members of the network have with an individual), and network structure, which encompasses properties such as size (number of alters in a network), degree (number of ties an alter has in a network) and density (interconnectedness among the alters).

In the introduction, I described the characteristics of international students (social demographic details such as gender and ethnicity) who are the focal individuals of the study. In this and the following chapter, I examine the relational characteristics, that is, the characteristics of ties between the focal individual and network members, such as each member's support provision and frequency of contact. I discuss the relational contents—such as the extent to which the network members play a role in the social lives of the students—along with the theoretical concepts. Theoretical considerations speculate that there is a specialisation of the relationship due to the geographical distance between respondents and alters. When relationships transcend national borders, so does the range of limits on support content. As there have been quite a few key terms discussed, the consecutive sections will tackle these terms in a detailed way one by one to give an overall picture of the background of the study.

2.2 Transcending Borders: An Overview

In a discussion round at one of the research group workshops, I found it intriguing when my colleagues shared their experiences and metaphorical objects linking to the topic of the discussion, 'what is transnational in our lives?' Most of the answers accounted for transnational practices and experiences such as "living abroad for a semester", "eating sushi prepared by a Polish chef", "my mobile phone", and "my adapter as it can be used in any country". Literally, how can the concept of transnationalism possibly be conceived? As a concurrent way of approaching the subject, I present a conglomeration of different perspectives on the theme, in the context of international students. In this study, I contend that being transnational means having relationships that transcend borders.

Transnational studies have contributed to a better understanding of a wide range of evolving social phenomena that take place across borders. The term as such has evoked a new perspective while examining certain processes or even a population. In general, transnationalism refers to increasing transborder relationships of individuals, groups, and organisations beyond state boundaries. Vertovec (2009) words it in an interesting way by seeing it as a condition in which, despite great distances and the presence of international borders, certain relationships have been comprehensively deepened, and now take place inconsistently in a global, yet common, virtual arena of activity. Transnationalism is inherently a part of the process of globalisation. Despite the usual comparisons with processes of diaspora and migration, transnationalism on a different level appears to be an eventual effect of these processes. A diaspora is the movement of people from a single geographical area to many, whatever the reason. Transnationalism proposes a view of how people have connections in two or more countries, for example, the home country and the new country in which they reside. They feel allegiances to both, wherein the nation state becomes less relevant. This allows people to establish themselves in a transnational space while still maintaining political, economic, and social ties to the society as a whole.

The beginning of sociological research dealing with mobility and migration was marked by a description of nation states as quasi-natural containers. This means that the nation state builds a container with a congruence of state authority, the people, and the territory (Faist 2009). An exclusive inclusion to the inside, for example through citizenship, and a closure to the outside, other nation states, strengthened this way of thinking. By defining the nation state as a container, the horizon of research fields was limited, and studies mostly focused on topics such as migration control and the integration of migrants. The golden era of this way of thinking was in the 1950s (Mau 2010), but criticism had become stronger by the early 1970s.

While people settled in a new country and made phone calls to their families back in their home country, it was only in the early 1990s that researchers in the social sciences embarked on exploring the concept of transnationalism as a basis for a new arena of study, in contrast to the foregoing discussions. In 1994, Basch along with Glick Schiller and Szanton-Blanc, who were pioneers in the field, defined transnationalism as "the process by which immigrants forge and sustain multistranded social relations that link together their societies of origin and settlement". This clearly denotes that social networks traversing across borders have been predominantly under focus in the theory of migrant transnationalism.

As in other domains involving human activities, transnationalism encompasses individuals, their networks of social relationships, and entrenched structures within the nation states. From the time of its inception, transnationalism has not only been evolving as a mere concept, but also its methodical framework has been in focus due to the inconsistencies posed by the co-existence of emergent globalisation processes (Appadurai 2001; Featherstone 1993) and the emphasis on the importance of nation states' "methodological nationalism" (Wimmer and Glick Schiller 2002). The coherent setting fabricated new theoretical ideas of how the networks of the individuals undergoing these processes through the move span national boundaries like transnational social fields (Glick Schiller and Fouron 1999), and transnational social spaces (Pries 2013; Faist 2004). These concepts overlook the aforementioned constraints and enable researchers to delineate the relationships between those who move, and those who stay behind but experience effects through their transnational fields.

The notion of a transnational field (Schiller et al. 1995) was primarily proposed as follows: migrants live within a "transnational social field" that includes the state from which they originated and the one in which they settled. A social field can be defined as a boundless territory of meshing egocentric networks. Molina et al. (2012a) emphasise Glick Schiller's reference to the Manchester School's work on social networks by pointing out Barnes' (1954) first usage of the term "social field" when talking about social networks. They explain that the implementation of the relational pattern to develop transnational theory inherited these ways of hypothesising and studying social relations. Following this proposition, "transnational social field" would embrace the personal network perspective, placing the analysis of transnational phenomena "from inside" in certain places, whereas "transnational social space" would adopt the whole network perspective, positioning the analysis from outside (ibid.). This proposes a social framework within which entities are located, events occur, and relations are pronounced. This complex social view of the social field provides a useful theoretical resource to understand the ongoing forms and consequences of international student mobility. These include challenges international students face in understanding their mobility, conveying the transnationality of their experiences, and positioning themselves advantageously in transnational social fields they themselves have helped create.

Based on the concept of a transnational social field, Mouw et al. (2014) tested immigrant transnationalism with data from both origin and destination communities, including the communication flow between the networks. Conceptualising the migration experience as taking place within social fields moves the analysis beyond those who migrate to those who do not necessarily move but are connected to migrants through the networks of social relations they sustain across borders. This insight is key, as it reveals that the impact of migration is not solely related to return. The behaviour, attitude, and perception of youngsters will vary, and it will be interesting to identify and study the differences with respect to social, political, and economic processes which lead to transnational formations after moving from one country to another.

The idea of transnational formations has emerged as a powerful new theoretical optic through which I explain the constitution of cross-border relationships and social formations that span across the world. It is linked to new practices of resource formation that disputably involve global bridging structures or networks that have essentially become incoherent from their national roots. In this sense, the idea of transnationalism proposes structures of ties, interactions, exchanges, and mobility that range across and span the world (Kennedy and Cohen 2007). The social formations are contrarily termed by Levitt and Glick Schiller (2004) as *forms of being* and *forms of belonging* that people merge in different practices within transnational social fields; they do not always happen concurrently. Central to the analysis of transnational social formations are the transnational relationships entwined in networks.

Distance Entailing the Lens of Transnationalism

Transnational relationships are ties spanning more than one country, in the broader sense, all relationships of an individual to persons who do not live in the same country, whether they are family or friends. In terms of social networks, when it comes to the operationalisation of "transnationalism", in this study I define transnational ties as either (1) the ego's ties to people in their home country or (2) the ego's ties to people in any country other than the country where they are currently living. Local ties are ties to people living in the same country as the ego when the interview is conducted. The differences in the transnationality of the personal networks can be explained by mobility patterns and by the duration of stay of the respondents in their current country of residence. The combined reflection upon mobility and specific personal characteristics, along with the transnational approach in personal networks, will provide a clear picture of the network dynamics. Before examining this area, it is also beneficial to have a closer look at the proportions within the two broad categories of transnationality: transnational and non-transnational ties. The main composition of students' network ties in terms of transnationality is as follows: out of 1474 alters, 936 are non-transnational ties (63.2 per cent), and the remaining 538 are transnational ties (36.8 per cent).

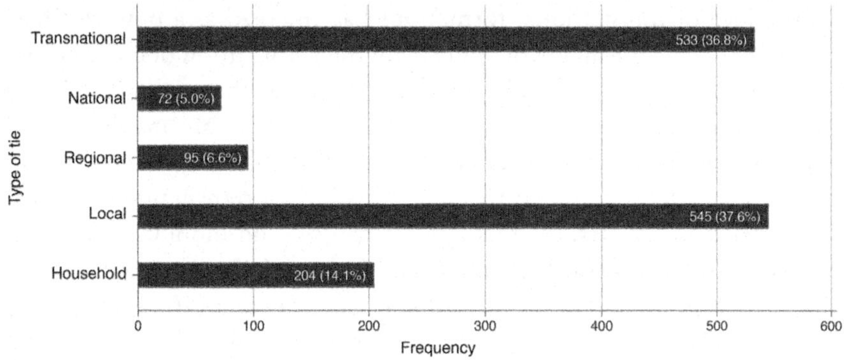

Fig. 2.1 Geographical distance of the alters

In this book, I categorise the geographical distance into five types: transnational, national, regional, local, and household (see Fig. 2.1). While the transnational category stands on its own, the other categories are encompassed under non-transnational ties. At the relational level, it is ascertained that there is a prevalence of local ties (around 37.6 per cent), as in ties living in the same city/town/neighbourhood. The second highest rank is for transnational ties (36.8 per cent), the pivotal category in the study, which encompasses ties living in another country from the ego. With just a 0.8 percentage point difference, both play a role in making up most of the international students' network. This will be dealt with more in Chap. 3 when viewing the composition of these ties at the network level. Although transnational ties are noteworthy, it must be kept in mind that non-transnational ties also have their share. For the remaining ties, the survey data shows there are 204 household ties (14.1 per cent), 95 regional ties (6.6 per cent) and 72 national ties (5 per cent). It can be seen that in the non-transnational ties, the majority of the ties live close to the ego in geographical terms. National ties, which are ties living in another state of the country from where the ego lives, are the least numerous.

Apart from this distinction, I studied transnational activities, that is, contact with people in the home country, frequency of socialising with people from the home country in the current country of residence as well as with other international people in the same country of residence, and home country visits. Most of the students travel to their home country less than five times a year (61 per cent). Contact with the home country is inversely proportional to visits to the home country, as there is an increase in contact with a decrease in visits. Almost 91 per cent of the respondents have weekly contact, with nearly half of them talking or staying in contact every day. Data shows that on a daily basis respondents tend to spend more time, and engage in activities more, with international people (54.7 per cent) than with people of the same origin (29 per cent).

The notion of home is no longer locatable with 'here' and 'there' but is re-conceptualised and supposedly imaginary. It covers models of both an abstract nostalgic past and an idealistic future (Wiles 2008). Sometimes it means a place where one tends to return for vacations, and other times it can be nostalgic and a part of childhood, as it includes time spent living there, the people one knew, the place one lived, and all those nostalgic moments. Nationality is not orientated anywhere, but tends to be dynamic. In my online pre-test and focused group interviews, some of the international students found the term "home country" to be tricky as they could not relate themselves to "home" in a straightforward way. One example is a Russian friend of mine who was born in Russia but moved to Germany at the age of seven. The questions on home country puzzled her, as her sense of belonging, when it comes to home country, is automatically driven to Germany, where she had most of her friends and childhood memories, but it is not really her country of origin. She still visits Russia every year to see her grandparents. It can be alleged that the whole concept of home country is affected by mobility. As the term "home country" is dealt with among a floating population in a transnational perspective which involves movement between borders, this necessitates asking whether their country of birth is their home country or not. The state or quality of belonging to, or being connected with, a nation by nativity or parental nationality is no longer compelling but is different from that, as seen in few cases in my pre-test.

Simply put, home country does not necessarily mean the country of birth but the country where students choose to identify their home. This also gives rise to the questions being definite because of the movement involved. This was overcome by asking whether the country of birth is the same as the home country. If that was not the case, then the country/countries that the respondent could relate to more as being their home country was asked for. While 88.8 per cent of the respondents consider their country of birth as their home country, the others chose other countries. It is noticeable that many respondents chose Germany and France as their home countries in first and second choice respectively, which draws out an assumption that migration took place here.

According to the destination-country statistics, a large number of the students are in the country for one or two years. At the same time, the decrease of respondents in the country for more than a year also implies that students tend to be more mobile, and do not really stay in one place for a long time. The reasons for the move were elicited through presenting options that offered possible motivations for going abroad, from the wider employment opportunities at home to the language of instruction. The most important reason for the move was the important or famous university, professor, area of study, or programme in their field. The second most important was related to wider employment opportunities abroad after graduation (19.6 per cent).

Being in different countries/places or having travelled to many countries entails gaining knowledge and also establishing and maintaining ties in those countries. This was covered through the question of whether the student had been abroad for more than three months before the current education. The mobility and reasons for the stay are again reflected in the specific personal characteristics of the sample. Over half (52.4 per cent) of the respondents had lived outside their home country before arriving in the current country of residence. The United States was the topmost destination among the respondents for being the place for the longest stay abroad (7.9 per cent), followed by Germany (7.3 per cent) and the Netherlands (4.5 per cent). Most of them had been abroad for the first time during 2009–2011, with the second visit in 2012. The purpose of stay for both was study related (28.1 per cent and 21.5 per cent respectively) and this concentration conveys that the distribution is pretty similar for being abroad for the second time.

2.3 The Shift from Networks to Communities

Given that there are different plausible intangible directions for the analysis of the content of transnational social formations, quite a few studies (Mazzucato and Schans 2011; Mouw et al. 2014; Molina et al. 2012b) have taken the network approach which has emerged in recent times. Dahinden (2009) followed a cross-cutting-ties approach, as she calls it, to study 250 migrants and non-migrants in a small Swiss city, Neuchatel. She found that transnationalism exhibited factors of social structures and social positions in which the individuals were embedded. This is inclined towards the early theorisation of personal community, that is, the network of relationships of people, which has also been recently used to describe and examine transnational social formations.

To provide a point of commencement for considering transnational social formations, the concept of community is taken into account from the perspective of social networks, which is already built with a strong base on the exertions of Wellman and his team. To set out the background of the term "community", I will first explore the definitions in the field. Wellman along with his colleagues (Chua et al. 2011) delineates three areas:

1. The traditional approach of viewing communities with a focus on specific geographical areas. This basically emphasises that community built is close and spatially bounded, and people know each other well.
2. Community is a collection of individuals or a group, which is characterised by a form of harmony and commonly shared values, norms, and interests.
3. Networks of relationships between individuals make up a community. Generally, this is less traditional due to the tremendous shift in the view of communities as being spatially defined to being relationally defined.

The third perspective—community as a social network which interprets shared relationships as a form of social environment—has been widely researched by Wellman and colleagues. As explained in the previous section, personal communities are defined as social networks consisting of an individual set of ties. From this standpoint, ties can be friends, neighbours, kin, colleagues, fellow members of a group, acquaintances, or even community members in an organisation. In the book *Virtual Communities: Bowling Alone, Online Together,* Felicia Wu Song (2009) contends that communities in general revolve around place, number of ties, and quality of interaction. Taking this into consideration, internet phenomena can be discerned as redefining community from traditional geographical spaces with face-to-face contact to virtual spaces with mediated interactions.

Looking back at the genesis of community, discussion started with the societal change experienced at the time of industrialisation and the rise of modern society by the end of the nineteenth century. Tönnies (1963) was one of the first to illustrate this change through the Gemeinschaft-Gesellschaft dichotomy. He argued that the gemeinschaft community consists of ties which were close and local, whereas gesellschaft consists of ties that were more coherent in nature, in the sense that interactions took place based on obligations and were far apart. While a few scholars like Durkheim (1964) recognised that people became more dependent on one another, Weber (1968) claimed that the industrialised world brought social isolation.

The conceptual benefits of the network perspective appear to be relevant for the adequate theorisation and operationalisation of social formations, especially in the transnational research context. Consequently, Wellman (1979) exerted the community concept for investigations involving proximity, with the help of the network analysis. He portrayed transformation of the community through this process, by treating the community as a social network rather than a place. This not only clarifies the terminology but also sheds a new perspective on how a localised, dense interweaving of patterns is thus a possible way of embedding people in a personal community. The question of who is within what kind of social structures, and the modes of relationship which maintain the exchanges of support and inclusiveness, is targeted at the individuals.

Tie strength was articulated by Granovetter (1983) as a fusion of duration, emotional intensity, mutual confiding, and reciprocal services which make the tie distinct. Marsden and Campbell (1984) verify the application of three of the proportions of tie strength, namely frequency of interaction, emotional intensity, and the intimacy of the relationship. It was found that the emotional intensity of the relationship most realistically signifies tie strength. The idea of emotional intensity proportional to the strength of the tie between two nodes is somewhat reasonable, as emotional intensity also assesses the notion of closeness. It is for this reason that closeness was measured and was one of the network instruments in the study. Socio-emotional closeness is a well-established and traditional measure in network studies especially when personal communities are in focus (Wellman 1979; Fischer 1982; Marsden and Campbell 1984; Boase 2006). Nearly 40 per cent of the ties mentioned by the international students are very close ones. Around 27 per cent of the ties are close and 21 per cent of the ties occupy the middle position of being somewhat close. While around five per cent were less close, only 2.2 per cent of the ties mentioned are supposed to be not close at all. This conforms with the concept of a personal community, and also affirms that a personal network study usually elicits a lower number of alters with a significant proportion of close ties.

The personal communities structured as proposed give a vivid explanation of relationships, which is required in order to explain key concepts of social networks in a conventional setting. This can be done more comprehensively by the introduction of the concept of structural analysis (Burt 1982; Wellman 1988). I elaborate in detail on the structure of social networks and relations between actors. The various types of structural analysis are perspicuously oriented to conceptualisations that appear cogent for personal communities as social networks. As such, they provide the basis for the understanding of personal communities in the context of migration and their transnationality. They are also intended to sharpen the understanding of social support in the social context. It is fundamental for a network theoretical approach that the characteristics of the relationships and the pattern of structuring the relationships and networks are used to understand and explain the social behaviour and mode of action of relations and networks (Wellman 1988). From the perspective of ego-centred networks, for which different theoretical concepts and description of characteristics can be considered (Hall and Wellman 1985), there are two fundamentally different levels of approach to social relationships and social structures: *relational* and *structural* perspectives. The former focuses on the relationship between the ego and the alter (generally two individuals), and the latter focuses on the relationships of more than two individuals.

Both levels of analysis will be used for the description and analysis of the networks of international students. The development of the notion of personal communities shifts the unit of analysis from society to interpersonal ties and networks (Wellman and Potter 1999). Through the operationalisation of the community as a personal community, social embeddedness is based on the interpersonal environment. This interpersonal environment comprises each individual embedded in social relationships, because of their personal community which has an effect on their behaviour and actions. This can be viewed from another perspective, that the community presents a discrete sphere for social interactions among relationships, thus leading to social life. Consequently, attitudes and beliefs are formed during interaction with other people. Quintessential goods and services in the form of aid or duty that are indispensable in everyday life are exchanged as well. It is apparent that personal community is regulated not only by rational and logistical functions but also by psychological and emotional functions. For all of their advantages, personal communities, being sources of constraints at times, can be described as a double-edged sword. So, it can be rightly said that the personal communities act as a pivot to the function of social support and acquiesce in the transmission of values and norms, social control or regulation of behaviour, or even stressful aspects.

The common discrepancy in the field of social sciences is the grouping of units explored on the basis of attributional characteristics, which targets the explanation of social phenomena of the meso and macro levels in individuals (Granovetter 1985). In contrast, when it comes to network research, the primary focus is on relationships between people and not on their attributes. Secondly, it can be said that the identities, roles, and expectations of the actors emerge in the social structure. The normative behaviour of individuals is explained by their positions in social networks (Emirbayer 1997; White et al. 1976). Not only the actions of the individuals but also dyads, that is, networks that consist of two actors, are shaped by social networks. Granovetter (1985) asserts that relationships are embedded in networks. The network concept is able to expand other social scientific concepts to substantiate or even replace them. Structural analysis focuses on the quantity of the structure and dynamics of relationships and networks. In short, I propose that the concept of personal community can be used to describe and analyse structural formations within the study of social support in the context of international student mobility.

2.4 Conception of Social Support

Having someone with whom you can share your happiness or to whom you can tell a secret may be important, but it might be equally important to have someone who knows how to fix a window or where one can find a job. Social support has a lot to do with everyday activities, from striking a conversation to sharing stuff. Vaux (1988) analogises it with the wind: "their presence is so ordinary as often to go unnoticed" in a metaphorical way. The role of relationships is interchangeable over time, and there is no particular definition of any relationship. It seems wholly conceivable that different people from different contexts and different surroundings possess different talents and resources, and would be helpful under different circumstances. There are some characteristics or features that make a relationship unique and irreplaceable. Social support as a network-based phenomenon has become a focus of research for nearly half a century. Over this time, it has been interconnected with other network-based but distinct social factors such as social cohesion, social integration, and social capital (Song et al. 2011). Social support and social networks are concepts that describe the structure, processes, and functions of social relationships.

There is a wide range of social relationships in terms of an individual's degree of social integration, and factors like marital status, contact with friends and relatives, and membership in certain organisations. Intimate relationships, which can be marked by the degree of closeness and strength, are important for one's well-being. The most intimate relationships and their availability can involve experiencing the delight of falling in love, making a new friend or losing a friend, and maybe the pain of lost love or the death of a family member (Vaux 1988). The definition of a personal relationship totally depends on the perspective of the individual who is defining and sharing it with another individual. In a sociological context, there are shared values and norms laid out for relationships. Despite the rigid setting, some relationships—like a friendly relationship between a professor and a student—can become indiscreet.

The intermediate level of social environmental ties, that is, social networks, represents a flexible compromise between the integration and intimacy approaches (Vaux 1988). This approach allows a broad range of social ties to be examined. Student networks are usually examined by categorising them according to friendship networks, as it is assumed that friends form the majority in students' networks (Bilecen 2014; McCabe 2016). Even though friends play a vital role in the provision of social support, it is pragmatic to also include family and other specific roles such as cousins, neighbours, and flatmates. The relational distribution of international students' networks shows that their networks are composed of a motley collection of ties. The mean percentages of ties in each role relationship are as follows: 40.5 per cent are friends, 14 per cent are nearest family (spouse [5.9] and parent [8.9]), 7.7 per cent are distant family (sibling [5.0], relative [2.1], and cousin [0.7]), 9.1 per cent are known from work (colleagues), 8.1 per cent are known from studying in the class (classmates) and 7.7 per cent live in the vicinity (flatmates [4.5] and neighbours [2.9]). The dominance of friends overall at the relational level is similar to the Connected Lives project (2006). It would be interesting to check the interconnectedness between the relationships belonging to different contexts and I will elaborate on this in detail in Chap. 3.

Taking a quick look at the history of social support, its roots developed almost a century ago at the time of the earliest works of sociology. Simmel (1902) noticed the change from personal and multidimensional relationships to impersonal and specialised relationships due to rapid industrialisation and urbanisation. It all begun with the social exchange theory, which considers that social relationships begin with the exchange of tangible and universal resources such as providing services (Homans 1961). They note that the same exchange when it happens between people who know each other is characterised and perceived differently. The distinctiveness of the exchange participants plays quite a vital role in the exchange and it is noted that there are higher levels of intimacy as the relationship progresses (Altman 1973). From this viewpoint it is evident that not all individuals are privileged and enjoy the benefits of getting support from others. There is an imbalance in that some might be within reachable distance to seek support from those willing to support, and others might be disadvantaged by not having many resources. It is plausible that they have little choice in terms of receiving support or giving support to someone. Social exchange theory also provides another outlook on the issue when one person gives support to another and expects to be treated in the same way. Caplan (1976) observes the noteworthiness of the reciprocity of relationships, coining the term "support system". It may turn out that the other person provides support, but there is also a possibility that the other person might not provide support as expected. To sum up, it is most likely that relationships require reciprocity over time, and that they thrive for a period of time. I look at the support system in students' social lives, that is, both the support received and that given.

Structure, composition, and relationship quality could be regarded as the main features of a support network. Following Wellman, Fischer (1982) found that after a decade the social ties of people living in urban and rural areas did not differ, including the quality of ties. Using the network perspective, Wellman and Fischer showed that social amendments accompanying industrialisation had altered communities without ruining them. Network analysis not only imparts a focus for research on social support but also plays a key role in facilitating a more complete understanding of support phenomena as they expand across geographical spaces. As relationships spread through different parts of the world—a phenomenon of the times we are living in—communication flows and channels should be tracked in order to study the support exchange. This gives an idea of how the networks are mediated, owing to the fact that support can be interpreted as the degree to which an individual's needs are catered to by dint of interactions.

Caplan et al. (1975) introduced the concept of social support, drawing distinctions between various different kinds of support. Although there are numerous kinds of support, I focus on four dimensions throughout the book: emotional, instrumental, and informational support, as well as social companionship[1] (Burt 1984; Cohen and Wills 1985; Cobb 1976). In response to the indefinite approach to social support and the outlined network assessment, a subset of the social network was elicited. All the social ties that are supportive are measured following the ego-centric network approach, using social network questions known as name generators to study social support exchange in the networks. Emotional support involves support from companions, letting a person know that they are accepted, and being there to share and talk, while social companionship is gleaned from togetherness, which may distract an individual from problems and help create a positive mood. Informational support signifies the transfer of pertinent information to help with a situation. Instrumental support includes actions and materials made available through an individual's system of support. Each dimension can be categorised further. For example, instrumental support can be small or large: borrowing money or tools for fixing a bed would be considered a smaller contribution, whereas moving to a new house or babysitting would be considered a greater contribution.

From the social exchange perspective, international students may have more or less value to offer: some students may be advantaged, with many resources and favourable exchange conditions, whereas others may have little to offer and have little choice but to engage in unfavourable exchanges with relatively unsatisfying relationships. Thus, social exchange theory provides another line of thought in social relationships and well-being. Most remarkably, it reminds us that the benefits derived from social relationships are distinct and may be of peculiar and circumstantial value, that relationships require reciprocity over time. Encounters with others are moulded to social forms in order to facilitate reciprocal exchanges. The role of reciprocity in social support exchanging behaviour is essential for determining the support provided by the network members to the ego/respondent. In this study, I define reciprocity as the sources of support reciprocated from the alter to the individual, considering the same dimensions of social support[2] which are used for the elicitation of the alters.

I discuss proportional distribution of relationships for each support dimension in international students' networks. The most common form of social support is emotional support, which is provided by nearly 48 per cent of the alters. Similarly, it ranks highest among the support given by the student to the relationships in their networks, accounting for about 57 per cent. The proportion of those who spend leisure time or pursue a hobby make up 44 per cent. Coming to informational support, which could be seeking information regarding the university or the host country, it contributes up to 29.6 per cent of the total support sought, and 42.3 per cent is given back by the student. The lowest proportion of all the support forms is instrumental support from the network members, in which money is borrowed or practical help is provided (27.8 per cent). Out of the support dimensions given by the ego, instrumental support is the least, accounting for around 29.6 per cent. Although the alters were elicited through the name generators, not all the members in the networks are support-providing contacts. In the instrument there was a prompt question after the name generators, and it was found that 16.7 per cent of the alters in the international networks do not provide support.

Caring for someone can provide mutual emotional support, and even investing time in a relationship with a particular person is a form of support. Cobb (1976) proposes that social support is a subjective perception in which the individual feels "that he is cared for and loved, that he is esteemed and valued; that he belongs to a network of communication and mutual obligation." This quotation subtly emphasises the importance of reciprocity and the availability of resources through the flow of communication between individuals. This might be explained by a meet-up among a group of friends at a high school alumni party. Six out of eight classmates who were close in school stayed in touch and met regularly after school life. The other two friends who were not in contact felt left out when the other six turned up for the party in matching costumes. This illustrates the advantageousness of maintaining an active communication flow in the network.

Social support, one of the elements of shared social ties, can be evaluated through the type of activity involved, and also the type of contact between the individuals. This gives rise to questions such as: How can the characteristics of the students' networks be related to the social support received and given? Do they vary across individual types of social support? Can the differences in social support exchange be explained merely by demographic details or by a combination of both students' individualistic and network characteristics? I elaborate in detail and try to answer these questions in Chap. 5. I now turn to another key query: What are the media channels and what is the frequency with which they are used to engage in social activities? In discussing the media use and frequency through concepts such as co-presence and multiplexity, I continue to develop the framework of the study.

Notes

1. The four different network generators measuring four different types of social support were as follows:

    1. Emotional support
    Whom did you discuss important personal matters with in the last three months (for example, talking with someone when you were depressed, explaining your problems, or expressing your happiness)?

    2. Instrumental support
    Who are the people you asked for help in the last three months (for instance, to borrow a small amount of money or a household item, or even to ask for help with small jobs like photocopying or taking care of the house when you're absent)?

    3. Informational support
    Who are the people you have asked for advice in the last three months (for instance, asked assistance in accessing information, asked opinion or information regarding your stay or shared professional decisions)?

    4. Social companionship
    Who are the people you enjoyed socialising with in the last three months (spent time chatting, played games, went for a walk, watched a video/movie, or even pursued a hobby)?

2. The question used to elicit reciprocal support ties: I would like to know how important you were in his/her life and whether you helped or provided support. Here are some activities/situations.

    Name 1 .... discussed/shared a personal matter with me
    Name 1 .... borrowed money or sought practical help from me
    Name 1 .... asked my opinion in making an important decision
    Name 1 .... socialised/spent leisure time with me

References

Altman, I. (1973). Reciprocity of interpersonal exchange. *Journal for the Theory of Social Behaviour, 3*(2), 249–261.

Appadurai, A. (Ed.). (2001). *Globalization* (Vol. 2). Duke University Press.

Barnes, J. A. (1954). Class and committees in a Norwegian island parish. *Human Relations, 7*(1), 39–58.

Bilecen, B. (2014). *International student mobility and transnational friendships.* Palgrave Macmillan.

Boase, J. (2006). The strength of Internet ties. In *Pew Internet & American life project.*

Burt, R. S. (1982). *Toward a structural theory of action: Network models of social structure, perception, and action.* Academic Press.

Burt, R. S. (1984). Network items and the general social survey. *Social Networks, 6*(4), 293–339.

Campbell, K. E., & Lee, B. A. (1991). Name generators in surveys of personal networks. *Social Networks, 13*(3), 203–221.

Caplan, G. (1976). The family as a support system. In G. Caplan & M. Killilea (Eds.), *Support system and mutual help: Multidisciplinary explorations* (pp. 19–36). New York: Grune and Stratton.

Caplan, R. D., Cobb, S., & French, J. R. (1975). Relationships of cessation of smoking with job stress, personality, and social support. *Journal of Applied Psychology, 60*(2), 211.

Chua, V., Madej, J., & Wellman, B. (2011). Personal communities: The world according to me. In J. Scott & P. J. Carrington (Eds.), *The SAGE handbook of social network analysis* (pp. 101–115). Thousand Oaks, CA: Sage.

Cobb, S. (1976). Social support as a moderator of life stress. *Psychosomatic Medicine, 38*(5), 300–314.

Cohen, S., & Wills, T. A. (1985). Stress, social support, and the buffering hypothesis. *Psychological Bulletin, 98*(2), 310.

Dahinden, J. (2009). Are we all transnationals now? Network transnationalism and transnational subjectivity: The differing impacts of globalization on the inhabitants of a small Swiss city. *Ethnic and Racial Studies, 32*(8), 1365–1386.

Durkheim, E. (1964). *The Division of labour in society.* New York: Free Press.

Emirbayer, M. (1997). Manifesto for a relational sociology. *American Journal of Sociology, 103*(2), 281–317.

Faist, T. (2004). Social space. In G. Ritzer (Ed.), *Encyclopedia of social theory* (pp. 331–332). Thousand Oaks, CA: Sage.

Faist, T. (2009). Transnationalization and development: Toward an alternative agenda. *Social Analysis, 53*(3), 38.

Featherstone, M. (1993). Global and local cultures. In J. Bird et al. (Eds.), *Mapping the futures: Local cultures, global change* (pp. 169–187). London and New York: Routledge.

Fischer, C. S. (1982). *To dwell among friends: Personal networks in town and city.* University of Chicago Press.

Fischer, C. S. (1984). *The urban experience.* Harcourt.

Granovetter, M. (1983). The strength of weak ties: A network theory revisited. *Sociological Theory*, 201–233.

Granovetter, M. (1985). Economic action and social structure: The problem of embeddedness. *American Journal of Sociology, 91*(3), 481–510.

Hall, A., & Wellman, B. (1985). Social networks and social support. In S. Cohen & L. Syme (Eds.), *Social support and health.* New York: Academic Press.

Hanneman, R. A., & Riddle, M. (2011). Concepts and measures for basic network analysis. In J. Scott & P. J. Carrington (Eds.), *The SAGE handbook of social network analysis* (pp. 340–369). Thousand Oaks, CA: Sage.

Hogan, B. (2009). From each according to media? Testing Wellman's theory of networked individualism.

Homans, G. C. (1961). *Human behavior: Its elementary forms.* New York: Harcourt, Brace, and World.

Kennedy, P. M., & Cohen, R. (2007). *Global sociology* (p. 550). New York University Press.

Levitt, P., & Schiller, N. G. (2004). Conceptualizing simultaneity: A transnational social field perspective on society. *International Migration Review, 38*(3), 1002–1039.

Marsden, P. V., & Campbell, K. E. (1984). Measuring tie strength. *Social Forces, 63*(2), 482–501.

Mau, S. (2010). *Social transnationalism: Lifeworlds beyond the nation-state.* Routledge.

Mazzucato, V., & Schans, D. (2011). Transnational families and the well-being of children: Conceptual and methodological challenges. *Journal of Marriage and Family, 73*(4), 704–712.

McCabe, J. M. (2016). *Connecting in college: How friendship networks matter for academic and social success.* University of Chicago Press.

McCarty, C., Gamper, M., Lubbers, M., & Molina, J. L. (2011). Migration and networks. In G. A. Barnett (Ed.), *Encyclopedia of social networks* (Vol. 1). Sage.

McEwen, R. N. (2010). *A world more intimate: Exploring the role of mobile phones in maintaining and extending social networks* (Doctoral dissertation).

Molina, J. L., Petermann, S., & Herz, A. (2012a). *Defining and measuring transnational fields*. Institut zur Erforschung Multireligiöser und Multiethnischer Gesellschaften.

Molina, J. L., Lozares, C., & Lubbers, M. J. (2012b). The geographical distribution of the personal networks of people living in Catalonia: A dual society. *GRAFO Working Papers, 1*, 1–19.

Mouw, T., Chavez, S., Edelblute, H., & Verdery, A. (2014). Binational social networks and assimilation: A test of the importance of transnationalism. *Social Problems, 61*(3), 329–359.

Pries, L. (Ed.). (2013). *New transnational social spaces: International migration and transnational companies in the early twenty-first century*. Routledge.

Schiller, N. G., Basch, L., & Blanc, C. S. (1995). From immigrant to transmigrant: Theorizing transnational migration. *Anthropological Quarterly*, 48–63.

Schiller, N. G., & Fouron, G. E. (1999). Terrains of blood and nation: Haitian transnational social fields. *Ethnic and Racial Studies, 22*(2), 340–366.

Simmel, G. (1902). The number of members as determining the sociological form of the group. I. *American Journal of Sociology, 8*(1), 1–46.

Song, F. W. (2009). *Virtual communities: Bowling alone, online together*. Peter Lang.

Song, L., Son, J., & Lin, N. (2011). Social support. In J. Scott & P. J. Carrington (Eds.), *The Sage handbook of social network analysis* (pp. 116–128). Thousand Oaks, CA: Sage.

Thoits, P. A. (1982). Conceptual, methodological, and theoretical problems in studying social support as a buffer against life stress. *Journal of Health and Social Behavior*, 145–159.

Tönnies, F. (1963). *Community and Society*. New York, NY: Harper & Row. Gemeinschaft und. Gemeinschaft, originally published in German, 1887.

Vaux, A. (1988). *Social support: Theory, research, and intervention*. Praeger Publishers.

Vertovec, S. (2009). *Transnationalism*. Routledge.

Weber, M. (1968). Economy and society. In *Conceptual exposition* (Vol. 1, pp. 956–1005).

Wellman, B. (1979). The community question: The intimate networks of East Yorkers. *American Journal of Sociology, 84*(5), 1201–1231.

Wellman, B. (1988). The community question re-evaluated. In M. P. Smith (Ed.), *Power, community and the city* (pp. 81–107). New Brunswick, NJ: Transaction Books.

Wellman, B. (1992). Which types of ties and networks provide what kinds of social support. *Advances in Group Processes, 9*(1992), 207–235.

Wellman, B. (2011). Studying the Internet through the ages. In M. Consalvo & C. Ess (Eds.), *The handbook of Internet studies* (pp. 17–23). Chichester: Blackwell Publishing Ltd.

Wellman, B., & Potter, S. (1999). The elements of personal communities. In B. Wellman (Ed.), *Networks in the global village* (pp. 49–82). Boulder, CO: Westview Press.

White, H. C., Boorman, S. A., & Breiger, R. L. (1976). Social structure from multiple networks. I. Blockmodels of roles and positions. *American Journal of Sociology, 81*(4), 730–780.

Wiles, J. (2008). Sense of home in a transnational social space: New Zealanders in London. *Global Networks, 8*(1), 116–137.

Wimmer, A., & Glick Schiller, N. (2002). Methodological nationalism and beyond: Nation–state building, migration and the social sciences. *Global Networks, 2*(4), 301–334.

3

New Agency of Personal Communities

3.1 Media as the Agency

New gadgets and technologies are introduced every now and then. Thanks to the newsfeed on Facebook and Twitter, users stay informed about world issues in addition to being informed about friends' lives. I communicate with my friends via WhatsApp regularly and use Skype to call my family at least once a week. The fact that media use influences my social life and is experienced as part of the composition of my everyday life is clearly visible. But with the outwardly constant explosion of new media technologies, one wonders if it is feasible to discontinue the use of these technologies as it affects the practice of maintaining ties in everyday life. The continuous development of the media landscape accounts for variations in media usage trends including, for example, the recent Facebook privacy crisis. The shift from one particular media platform to another can also be a factor influencing the pattern of media usage, such as the use of Orkut (a social networking site powered by Google) and MySpace, which once had numerous young students as its users before the widespread use of Facebook worldwide. It might also depend on lifestyle preference, for example the choice of not owning a smartphone or tablet, or even external factors such as the digital divide.

R. Kanagavel, *The Social Lives of Networked Students*,
https://doi.org/10.1007/978-3-319-96199-6_3

Despite the fact that the concept of social networks equips us with a more comprehensive understanding of human interaction than the concept of community (Costa 2006), the focus is mainly on personal communities, as the personal networks elicited are small and quite strong. In general, personal community ties are maintained both online and offline, with relationships formed online spilling into the physical realm and ties in the physical realm continuing as online interactions (Wellman and Haythornthwaite 2008).

More recently, the notion of transnational communities has replaced the old concept of migration as severing social ties. Prior to the internet, migration over long distances meant a disruption of the relationships in one's personal community because visits and continuous contacts were expensive and slow (Hiller and Franz 2004). Although we often deal with media queries about the isolated nature of the media, research has made it clear that the internet is in fact seamlessly integrated with personal communities and is rarely a separate second life in itself (Veenhof et al. 2008; Quan-Haase et al. 2002).

When talking about personal communities and provision of support, the subject of virtual communities pops up, and this must be discussed as well. In the case of forums, support might be received and given through communicating with weak ties that rely on online contact. The focus here is rather on personal communities, which will open up the question of giving support to weak ties, dealt with in internet research for some time. Although virtual communities (Rheingold 2000) are used for this kind of support exchange, it is probable that people—international students in particular—reach out using different media according to their affordances, to maintain contact with the members of their network. Regardless of the original location in which they are based, the internet supplies ample opportunity to access information as well as actively participate in social activities. In their book *Connected* Rainie and Wellman (2012) call this phenomenon a "triple revolution", comprising the internet, mobile, and social network revolutions. They reappraise the theory of networked individualism (Wellman et al. 2002), of how people are in charge of their personal communities at the hands of communication technologies as social affordances. While social affordances play their part, the media used can also be contingent on the personal cues (Hogan 2009) of the individuals, which I discuss in more detail in Chap. 4.

The Internet Phenomenon

The upsurge of new communication technologies not only facilitates but also augments communication activities. The internet today is part of our everyday lives. It provides traction not only for new relationships but also for the extension of ties, be they weak or strong. The internet has been researched extensively, covering various topics, and explanations are made depending on the people researched and methodology adapted. Though circumstances and geographical features influence people to a certain extent (Haythornthwaite 2005), this study will overlook this particular aspect, considering the specific international student population targeted. It has been estimated that there are 3,904,238,355 internet users,[1] which account for nearly half of the world's population. Today, the truth is the scenario portrayed by the famous internet meme of Maslow's hierarchy of need,[2] with Wi-Fi at the very bottom. This reflects the fact that many of us are not capable of surviving without the internet, and that it plays an integral role in our everyday lives.

Although the use of the internet is a global phenomenon, the way it is used by people, especially students, is perceived to be different in every place. With the advent of Web 2.0, the internet has become a lot more exciting and stimulating in the research arena, as young people seek to have more interactive communication and have become producers of content rather than mere consumers. The interactive usage of social media is changing the way in which people communicate and comprehend. The tacit reach of social media can be discerned through activities such as inviting a host of friends to a birthday party or organising a flash mob by creating a Facebook event. An evening spent by Brandon Stanton, Humans of New York (HONY) Facebook page owner, at Connaught Place in New Delhi can best exemplify the power of social media. While on his 50-day UN trip through 10 countries, Brandon made a stop in Delhi and a post on Facebook conveyed the time and place of his presence. Within exactly one hour, nearly 300 Indians had gathered to meet him personally and to show appreciation for his blog. The online photo blog about people living in New York City has provided an opportunity to build a global communication base that links people around the world. This demonstrates the level of connectedness spanning from home to a global scale after the advent of the internet.

Factors Affecting Media Preferences

There have always been debates on how the integration of media technologies in everyday life makes us antisocial. The effects of new media have been accused of leading to social isolation (Turkle 2011), but the debates have yielded inconsistent and ambiguous results. There is also another round of discussions on whether or not online and offline worlds should be regarded as separate. As mentioned earlier, this book overlooks those discussions and takes a completely new way of strategising the connection between media use and social interactivity. While the internet facilitates the enlargement of the geographical boundaries of social networks, it would be absurd to discuss whether media actually replace real-time communication and in-person experiences. This thinking does not only rely on the premise that there are definitive differences in talking to a person face-to-face and talking over Skype, but more on how it is perceived by the individual. This is where the question of whether media provides more social accessibility appears.

Social presence and computer-mediated communication is a vastly researched area in the field of educational sciences. Short et al. (1976) founded social presence theory, which became the groundwork for many theories on the effects of new media. They stated that social presence is the degree of salience between two communicators using a communication medium—that is, a person's cognizance of the presence of an interaction partner. This is crucial for the process by which an individual perceives other individuals, their characteristics, qualities, and inner states (Short et al. 1976). In the early stages, the focus was more on telecommunications. With the proliferation of the internet from the early 1990s, which implicitly influenced the relational view of social presence, computer-mediated communication studies evolved along with concepts of social cues and social effects. Along the same lines, Daft and Lengel's (1986) media richness theory postulates that media can be arranged on a continuum from lean to rich, based on the feedback, channel, and language used (Flanagin and Metzger 2001). While these theories highlight users' regard for media aspects, shared ideas and experiences are imperative in choosing and using media as well. Markus (1994) resonates with the idea that media richness theory is capable of predicting perceptions and use of older communication technologies, but new media is less reliable. On the contrary, it is conceivable that the new technologies can easily be consumed by the easy adaptation facilities. One good example is the shift from Facebook to Instagram for posting pictures.

While uses and gratifications theory (Katz 1959) explains how different people use the same media messages for different purposes to satisfy their psychological and social needs and achieve their goals, dependency theory (Ball-Rokeach and DeFleur 1976, 1989) posits an essential relationship among audiences, media, and the larger social system. Media theorists used the term "audience" when referring to people, as until the twentieth century people were really an audience, content was received and agenda-setting prevailed. This is evident when an individual seeks a certain medium to attain a certain goal, for example browsing through the internet for a recipe instead of watching MasterChef. Dependency theory envisages that one has to depend on media information to meet certain needs and achieve certain goals, similar to uses and gratifications theory. But on the contrary, one does not depend on all forms of media equally. Two factors have also been proposed which influence the degree of media dependence. First, a person will become more dependent on a medium that meets a number of needs than on a medium which provides a few. This is the key concept behind the increased usage of smartphones. Nowadays it has become clear that there is a demand for these devices, especially among students, which helps them to be wired on the go. One can send a WhatsApp message, post a photo on Snapchat, check Facebook notifications, and Viber call their friend all at the same time. Social stability being the second source of dependency can be demonstrated by the reliance on media for information during times of conflict. Although this is related to print and traditional media, or aimed at society as a whole, it is viewed through an individualistic lens concerning how certain platforms are reviewed and new choices made.

Flanagin and Metzger (2001) contend that media which once meant being less socially present and which needed gratification now appear to be considered rich multifunctional channels capable of most tasks once provided only by more traditional media. Despite the above theories, there is still a lack of a comprehensive understanding of the motives behind students' use of certain media channels in today's multifaceted setting. Does the potential selection of chosen media by individuals depend on the medium itself? Or is it considered according to the distance and mobility of where the person resides and uses the media to connect with members of the network? Media consumption habits and preferences vary notably from individual to individual. Hence there is a need to work out how far this influences the networks and makes it essential to segregate and explore why students prefer and interact with different media.

Media Convergence for Diverging Ties

The increase in geographical distance could possibly reduce the degree of social relationships and contacts, and particular forms of interaction are exhibited. Wellman and Wortley (1990) assert this assumption, declaring that proximity facilitates relationships. Does this facilitation lead to the maintenance of networks? Monge and Contractor (2001) use the same verb, pointing out that "proximity facilitates the likelihood of communication by increasing the probability that individuals will meet and interact". This gives the impression that proximity is an elementary factor essential to the formation of new ties in the network.

The power of media to shrink physical space while simultaneously expanding social space was foreseen decades ago. Even before the advent of the internet, McLuhan and Fiore (1967) hypothesised the emergence of a *Global Village* where physical distance would no longer be a hindrance to staying connected. Today the *Global Village* is becoming a reality. On one hand, there is a tremendous increase in population comprehended worldwide, while on the other hand, as the theory of six degrees of separation suggests, every person is separated from any other person on earth by only six links, a notion considered to be one of the prominent findings in social network analysis, which reminds us that we live in a small world. In a study conducted by Facebook and the University of Milan (2011), it was found that the average number was not six but actually 4.74, revealing that the distance seemed to be shrinking.

In the study of distance and the internet, Mok and Wellman (2007) identify differences in the frequency of interaction for different social relationships. The most frequent meetings take place between immediate family, while friends and acquaintances are subordinate to this. The lowest frequency of priority is contacting distant relatives. With the increase of the geographical distance between two people, it is assumed that contact information and interaction frequency gradually decrease (Mok and Wellman 2007). People who live close to each other have a diversity of options available to contact each other. At the same time, this does not mean that everyone is constantly in touch with each other. It is agreed by most people, though, that face-to-face contact seems to be easier to implement. Moreover, for technical and cost reasons, less distance might favour the side of having relationships in the immediate geographical environment, which in turn makes communication through mobile phones easier and faster. This might have been true three decades back, but today the statement is losing its significance with the proliferation of smartphones where messages are sent instantly.

Relationships that have a strong foundation of trust and love are more likely to adapt to staying connected no matter the circumstances, and the efforts are tremendous in this case, with the ties maintained through abounding and interconnected media. This interconnectivity of using a variety of media is known as media convergence (Jenkins 2006) or polymedia (Madianou and Miller 2013). Jenkins (2006) defines media convergence as the "flow of content across multiple media platforms", whereas polymedia refers more to the context of interpersonal communication. Strong ties are maintained through this connectedness, with people's digital social lives at their fingertips—another affordance of mobile technology. It is more natural to use different media to connect with people: from microblogging to FaceTiming with strong ties, while with weaker ties, discussion lists or social networking sites are preferred (Gruzd and Haythornthwaite 2013). Some relationships are so regularly engaged that it does not necessitate staying connected through all available media, and there is less reason to overcomplicate the use of multiple media channels.

The ability to access other communication channels such as Skype and email overcomes the barrier of maintaining transnational relationships. How far is it important for social lives? Does the importance diminish when the media used provide more stretch? The quality of social ties is independent of the place in which the relationship was established (online or face-to-face), of the geographical location, or even of the peer group. Other factors such as duration and content of the relationship might matter, along with network dimensions such as homogeneity. I describe these aspects of the networks in relation to transnationality in the next chapter.

3.2 Is Co-Presence Necessary?

Social presence highly depends on the quality of a communication medium, as there is a differentiation in text, audio, and video communication which is related to the sense of personal perception. We are social beings and co-presence plays a vital role in the thesis of media use. It shows subtle significance in a detailed exploration of the topic, even though it may seem explicit. According to social presence theory, communication is efficient if the communication medium has the appropriate social presence essential for the level of interpersonal participation necessary for a task. In the field of social presence, the face-to-face medium is considered to have the most social presence, while written, text-based communication has the least. It is presumed in any interaction between two people that the participants in the interaction are concerned both with enacting certain roles and evolving or preserving some sort of personal relationship.

Some researchers have proposed that intimacy and immediacy are subsidising factors to social presence. According to Tu (2002), social presence is primarily based on three dimensions: social context, online communication, and interactivity. Most studies focus on this in relation to online learning environments. In their study on social presence, Tu and McIsaac (2002) state that social presence has a positive effect on online instruction in terms of learning, but that, even so, frequency of participation does not symbolise high social presence. This can be tested with the definition of frequency of activity proposed by Hogan (2009), where he states that strategies for action refer in large measure to habits, be it contacting a person by email or having a mobile chat. While social presence theory proposes this, Antony Giddens (1990) contrarily uses the term "pure" relationship to describe relationships based on mutual sharing of thoughts and feelings. According to Giddens, the mutual agreement between individuals to perpetuate the relationship makes it "pure". Although I will not go deep into the psychological side of Giddens' definition, I remark that in sum and substance he emphasises that the intimacy is developed within oneself rather than the body being involved in it.

The way the relationship is perceived and the way the network is visualised in the human brain—the actual process—could lead to denaturalisation of the body. While there are studies dealing with this construct and the difference between body and presence, this study will not delve deeply into this except for when talking about the need to communicate. Even if bodies are present, the communication must be mediated. Social relationships in sociological processes change when the person is not present. Somehow, in the process, bodies are deconstructed, and the social processes are taken into account. This could also be said to play a vital role in the routinisation and imaginary nature of networks resulting in generating new space. A friend who is currently studying abroad highlights this well, reporting that in her weekly Skype sessions with her family, which are held on Sundays after their return from church, she knows exactly where each family member sits during the Skype session.

Face-to-face communication is also mediatised by routines. Human communication is more than mere talking or exchanging ideas. This process of communication is happening even when the other person is not present. In a parallel world, imagine there are no technologies and people stay close with their local ties and, if they go abroad, eventually lose their old ties. Even in that case, presence would not be the same. Movement does not replace feelings or forget the processes or other dynamics within the relationship. Furthermore, communication cannot just take place with the people whom one meets every day and with people living nearby. In as much as you are living together, your flatmate does not necessarily enjoy the benefits of friendship. Likewise, it is explicable that presence is not always good. Although relationships are digitally mediated, they somehow end up simultaneously having a face-to-face history. Manual Castells (2000), who proposed the network society, linked the rise of the internet with a pattern of forming relationships that Wellman subsequently described as "networked individualism" (Jamieson 2013). I contend that although Castells and Wellman make a clear-cut explanation of the shift from close-bound ties to far-flung ties and their mediation, the lack of pertinence of face-to-face personal relationships prevails.

3.3 Media Use and Frequency

At the ego level, individual characteristics of international students in terms of using three important media devices—which have been focused on in research for a long time—were collected. Personal desktops or laptops are more convenient for the conducting of personal affairs, which is not feasible or even affordable on a shared general computer. In general, students need a laptop or a desktop at home for study purposes. It can be time-consuming not to have a personal laptop/computer (travelling and going to the library at special times when computers are accessible), as this would require being dependent on the university library system. To stay connected with family and friends and having the luxury of staying connected at all times through the use of the internet, people depend on a smartphone, which is more personal, handy, and easy to carry around—offering 4G and Wi-Fi facility. Nearly three quarters of the students possess a smartphone on which they access the internet (70.2 per cent) and almost all of them (96.7 per cent) access the internet through their desktop/laptop/tablet.

The landline phone, which has the lowest percentage of usage (13.6 per cent), is mainly used to make calls to another landline for a cheaper rate, and is not usually used for long conversations. It is common that a landline telephone is not necessary if abroad for a short stay, as it is contract bound. The installation requires time and money if the student plans to stay for a long time, but on the other hand they are also more likely to share a flat where there is already a connection. I presume that people who stay for more than a year would prefer to have a landline connection. If there is a landline connection, it is generally shared in a flat, where it goes hand in hand with an internet connection.

Internet flat rates work when coupled with landline rates. When there are established contacts or relationships in the residing country, it is beneficial to have a landline connection at home to make free calls. On the other hand, a landline connection when used in a family household setup is a different circumstance from a shared flat as it is not personal. I am reminded of my days as a teenager, when I used to talk to a friend for hours during the night, causing disturbance for the whole family. This is where mobile phones' affordance of being more personal than landline phones comes in.

Mobile phones are proficient for making appointments/plans to meet someone who is living in the vicinity. Texting someone from a mobile phone totally depends on the network contract. It could be cheaper or more expensive than making quick phone calls. There is also the chance of making free calls if the other person also uses the same network. Using a mobile phone for making phone calls to people living abroad relates to the concept of media convergence in terms of how the smartphone encompasses most of its function within one device. It is possible to connect with a friend abroad at a cheaper rate using an app than actually calling a friend who lives in the same neighbourhood. The only essential thing for this is an internet connection and number registration. For example, with my German number registered on SmartVoip, I can make calls to the US for free and calls to India for one cent per minute, but a call made to a landline in Germany would cost me eight cents per minute. For this I prefer calling directly from a mobile connection without using the internet. Texting is used to contact local ties as it allows sending short messages. The only drawback is that certain network providers impose character limit for text messages which could cost double when the character limit exceeds 140.

When the use of certain apps is coupled with the use of the network, there is again relevance to the devices used by students nowadays. This is the standing of the social affordances of media channels experienced today. Tethering connection between Apple products is a good illustration of the procedure, and communication between the devices is also easily afforded on another level (for example the facilitation of sending free iMessages, FaceTiming, or sharing pictures via Airdrop on a Mac/iPad/iPhone).

Internet Access

In 2010, Facebook conducted a study on friendship connections, and I found the image intriguing as one can see borders of countries vividly, as delineated by the span of friendship connections, even though borders were not actually marked. This picture lucidly signifies the fact that media, specifically social networking sites, help in establishing transnational social ties. While the explosion of the internet opens up a window of opportunity for strengthening and expanding transnational activities for social interaction, new digital technologies establish inequalities in access. People from certain parts of the world are excluded from this opportunity because of the digital divide. While it is safe to assume that students' accessibility is not influenced, new perspectives can be shown by testing across different geographical regions, as most of the categorisation occurs between North America and rest of the world, or between developed and developing countries (Chen 2010; Fong et al. 2001).

In the study, most international students use the internet every day (97.9 per cent) and the rest use it several times a week. With regard to internet access, it can be observed that the time spent on the internet has been used to segregate individuals into heavy users and less heavy users according to their internet use (Boase 2008). Students use internet predominantly for a maximum of five hours (15 per cent). Comparing internet use among the geographical regions where students reside, I found that students studying in the Americas and Oceania spend the highest number of hours on the internet, with a mean of 8.3 and 7.3 hours respectively.

Classification

Media consumption habits and preferences vary notably from individual to individual. There is therefore a need to figure out how far this influences the networks, making it essential to segregate by use, and to explore why students prefer and interact with different media. The increase in smartphone use precisely conveys the general trend of burgeoning technologies, and demonstrates the degree to which students are consumers of this technology. 4G networks account for faster internet connectivity, which in turn facilitates regular use of email and social platforms. Having a smartphone makes one more organised and available for communication, allowing the individual to be online on the go.

Social support can be envisaged as multifaceted, flowing ceaselessly and simultaneously through numerous but interdependent channels. Depending on accessibility, support can be passed on by communication through chat, forums, blogs, mailing lists, groups, and message boards. The devices used for participation can be desktop systems or wireless media such as mobile phones and tablets. Apps which facilitate video chat and conferencing like Skype allow extra social cues in addition to chat and voice, whereas programs like social networking sites and emails—which are asynchronous—help in the exchange of resources and information despite temporal differences.

Be it networked individualism (Wellman 2001) or personal communication systems (Boase 2008), all communication processes involve the individual being at the centre and controlling the flow, while the procedure combines diverse media channels to connect with members in their own personal networks, rather than using them separately to connect with different social worlds. There is a degree of connectivity for every medium that involves the perception of the individual who is involved in the communication process. The strategies followed to maintain relationships and receive social support over long distances and the connection between social activities are examined according to the type of channel used. The different channels considered in the study are as follows:

- Face-to-face

  Since the proliferation of online media its role has been reduced, despite its prominence. In order to bring a balance, face-to-face contact was used as a separate category. Communicating personally or with a group depends largely on the context and the reason behind the communication. Apart from the sole purpose of communication, it is assumed that being there in person better enables care and help. Almost all of the ties are contacted by the ego in the network using this medium (95.2 per cent) and the frequency of meeting face-to-face with someone is positively correlated with many media channels like making phone calls (r = 0.26), texting (r = 0.35), emails (r = 0.11), instant messaging (known as IM) (r = 0.08), or social networking sites (abbreviated here as SNS) (r = 0.13), all at the level p = 0.01, and negatively correlated to other platforms (r = −0.21) and letters (−0.05).

- Letter
  Letters, the traditional form of communication which utilises the social cue of writing, can be considered more personal—because handwritten—than electronic forms of communication. Letters nowadays are replaced with greeting cards and postcards. Only 18.5 per cent of the ties are contacted by the students using this channel for communication, and the frequency and use of letters has a high level of positive correlation with emails (r = 0.17) and other platforms (r = 0.16) at p = 0.01.
- Phone call
  The introduction of this medium was a turning point for communication technology, starting from a location-based device having a local area network to a hand-held device. The frequency and use of phone calls is positively correlated to texting (r = 0.52)—which is highest among other media for phone calls, followed by emails (r = 0.27), IM (r = 0.31), SNS (r = 0.16), and other platforms (r = 0.20), all at p = 0.01 level. The correlation is perhaps accounted for by the fact that all of these channels can be accessed through mobile phones. Making phone calls is considered to be more personal as it allows one-to-one communication in spite of the fact that it facilitates conference calls as well. Phone calls rank the second highest (78.5 per cent) after face-to-face contact among different types of media use.
- Text
  This synchronous communication, which is helpful in dealing with different time zones and is personal as it is private, has added another string to the bow. The frequency of texting is positively correlated with emails (r = 0.26), IM (r = 0.26), and SNS (r = 0.27), which is high, and other platforms (r = 0.13), all at p = 0.01 level. Another important feature is that there is immediate communication in sending as well as receiving, given that the other person sees the message right away. It is observed that students who study abroad text

around 71 per cent of their alters, which is more than the usage of IM (62 per cent). The availability of the internet as a prerequisite for using instant messaging platforms can reduce this.

- Email
  Email is presumed to be the most important breakthrough in human communication, equal to the telegraph and telephone communication. The internet was recognised, and considered as a mode of communication, only after the first email exchange. The same kind of revolution arose after 2006 with the rapid spread and power of social media. Apart from the above-mentioned correlation with regard to email, frequency and email exchange is positively correlated to IM ($r = 0.13$) and other platforms ($r = 0.23$), all at $p = 0.01$ level. Bessiere et al. (2008) have found that email is used extensively to maintain geographically distant relationships with friends and family, and that women used it more than men. This raises the question of whether email acts as an easy communication tool for connecting transnational ties. Apart from the instant asynchronous control, another affordance emerges when email services and IM are integrated into a platform. A good example here is the Gmail account, where it is possible to see and chat with people who are online when opening the mail account. While chatting, if one person closes the window the other person can still open it and receive the message as an email.
- Instant Messaging
  The instant messaging platforms have been rarely used (Wellman et al. 2006) in previous studies as they were obscure. Instant messaging has become widely consumed these days, and the survey shows significant results when instant messaging was a separate option in the survey. It is also because of the increase in the use of smartphones that programs like WhatsApp, Signal, and Threema are particularly popular among the student population. WhatsApp also affords the usage of two numbers simultaneously: installation of a particular number on an app and registration of that number according to the country also facilitates the opportunity to enjoy the tariffs assigned to that particular country. The frequency and use of IM is positively correlated to SNS ($r = 0.50$) and other platforms ($r = 0.31$), all at $p = 0.01$ level.

- Social Networking Sites
  Tracing back the first examinations into online communities, Reid (1994) analysed play-based Multi-User Dungeon (MUD) virtual environments, Baym (1998) examined Usenet online groups and Rheingold (1985) explored the *Well* community. The *Well*, which began in 1985, stands as one of the first social networking websites. There is no allusion to social networks, but they discuss how relationships maintained offline are recreated online. With the explosion of social networking sites after the advent of Facebook, many studies have taken place among students. A comparative study (Quan-Haase and Young 2010) on gratifications derived from Facebook and instant messaging showed that Facebook was all about having fun and knowing about the social activities of others in one's social networks, whereas instant messaging is geared more towards relationship maintenance and development. Indeed, the very act of creating a profile on a social network site leads to content creation. This trend towards engagement has led to the development of a new term, *participatory media* (Jenkins 2006). As I am sitting in the library, I can see nearly seven out of ten people in the front rows checking their Facebook. The question *How frequently do you visit social networking sites?* had more variation in the categories of options, as these sites are frequented more on a daily basis. In the usual frequency categories, the option of "Daily" is the most common answer. I surmise that there is a variation between people who check Facebook once a day and three to five times a day, or even people who are on Facebook all day long. The most popular site used is Facebook (93.7 per cent) and, surprisingly, there was a huge gap between the first- and second-most-used sites. The other sites used are Twitter and G+, with 4.5 per cent and 1.8 per cent of the population using them, respectively.
- Other platforms
  The category *Other platforms* comprises platforms such as Skype, Viber, and FaceTime, which allow video conference calls. Nearly half of the alters are contacted via these platforms, for providing or giving support by the ego. The frequency and use of SNS is positively correlated to other platforms ($r = 0.27$), all at $p = 0.01$ level.

The Frequency Gauge

The measurement of media use is typically done by the partitioning of time, which is a necessity in the calculation. It involves the dimensions of social structuring of time: sequence, duration, temporal location, and recurrence (Zerubavel 1982). Here I consider the factor of frequency, both in terms of aggregated media use and media use with any individual in the network. Someone might regularly call their parents, but only do so at a specific time of the day for a specific duration, depending on the place they are living. In the case of international students, time difference poses barriers when contacting family or friends in their country of origin or any other country. One of the most precise means for representing activity is to use the diary-interview method. Michelson (2005) used the time-use diary technique to capture an intensive picture of an individual's day. Generally, in the diary-interview method, the respondent maintains a diary of their regular activities and contacts for a day or a week, in order to examine their day-to-day life. This is another instance that gives substance to the notion that online and offline activities are interwoven and not isolated incidents. For example, contacting my friend in London via WhatsApp is an usual everyday activity and not a separate task, as it occurs online.

It would be remiss to evaluate the data in this study using diaries, as one interacts with only a fraction of one's personal network on a given day or in a given week. On the contrary, I attempt to evaluate the far-reaching use of the many media of the respondent, as well as the wide-ranging media assessed and used for communication with a number of alters in the network as a whole. It is necessary to use basic and simpler categories. It is imperative to characterise the kinds of media use for a given individual. Time spent per day on the internet is not an exact measure of the time spent on the internet, since online activities vary significantly. They can be social activities such as email, instant messaging, or even gaming and work-related activities. That does not necessarily mean that adolescents use the internet most of the time for socialising, or that academics use only emails. Some individuals may spend a substantial amount of time having expressive conversations with a single alter, while others would be able to have many short instrumental conversations using the same amount of time using mobile phones. For this reason, the media-use measures in this study were elaborated in terms of frequency as well as type.

Transnational ties are contacted using mobile phones (both calls and text) several times a month on average, while non-transnational ties are contacted on average several times a week. A mobile is frequently used in the case of local ties because of expense, and also it is more common to use a mobile phone to follow up, make a short phone call to arrange a meeting, or quickly communicate something. For example, in the case of a close friend, it is natural or common to call that particular friend immediately, whether you are living in the same city or not. But somehow the connection of living in the same country gives an opportunity to contact that person more personally, while writing an email or a Facebook wall post is more likely to be used when that particular person is in another country. Use of all media (phone calls using mobile and landline as well as texting) at the individual level accounts for the highest percentage of use among non-transnational ties.

Media Multiplexity

Apart from the content of ties, the medium used to maintain the relationship can also be viewed from the perspective of multiplexity. The more contact is made by one communication medium, the more is made by others. There can be follow-ups from the use of one medium to another (Rainie 2006). Some social networks are more expressive and explicit than others, so that there are more opportunities to be more social, and some people might be more active through frequent communication in their networks. The idea of social affordances of technology can be used to give an understanding of why media multiplexity exists.

Talking about the relationship between use of one media channel and the use of other media channels, considering the frequency of media usage, and some demographic differences, media multiplexity looks at the likelihood of an individual using specific types and number of media channels based on their usage of one particular medium. The aspect of multiplexity also depends on the context and content of the tie. For example, if someone is a regular user of Snapchat as a means of communication, how likely is it that they will use Facebook as well? Does it make a person less likely to use the phone because they have replaced that form of communication with email? The study by Hogan (2003), based on the National Geographic Survey 2001, showed that individuals using the internet as a major form of communication are more likely to also use the phone or to meet someone in person. However, I find with myself, friends, and colleagues that people tend to have a preference for communication either overall or based on certain situations. I confer more about this in Chap. 5.

Nearly 98 per cent are media multiplex relationships, whereas two per cent are uniplex media relationships. Students use four to six channels to contact the highest number of relationships, accounting for approximately 18 per cent on average (Table 3.1). When interrelating the closeness factor with the number of media used by the respondent to connect with people in their networks, the closeness mean increases gradually with the increase in the number of media. International students connect with close ties (scale lies between *close* [three] and *very close* [four]) using five to eight types of media channels. This affirms the studies by Haythornthwaite (2000) and Koku et al. (2001), illustrating that stronger ties use more means of communication. Strong tie networks are supported through mandated media and other optional—more private—means of communication, such that the social support comes

Table 3.1 Media multiplexity for relationships

Number of media used	*n*	%	
1	36	2.5	Uniplex: 2.5
2	92	6.4	Multiplex: 97.5
3	157	11	
4	231	16	
5	262	18.1	
6	306	21.1	
7	256	17.7	
8	103	7.1	
Total	1443	100	

along with it as a whole package. They assimilate harmoniously to existing media, and modify new media according to local norms. Whatever the media change, the strong tie network, unlike the weak tie network, is likely to remain intact.

As the number of media channels used increased, it was observed that the number of support dimensions exchanged increased as well. However, individuals connected with alters using a variety of media channels (media multiplexity) did not really contribute much to increased support exchange.

Even with the innovation of technology and introduction of new technologies, after a while it is noteworthy that people familiarise themselves and stay up to date. This can be compared with the period when the internet started flourishing, or even the launch of Facebook. But there are also exceptions like Google+: although the promotion was enthralling, people turned it down and continued to use Facebook. In spite of the constant change in the media background, networks with strong ties remain unchanged as they are usually supported through personal means of communication in addition to the regular media channels used.

3.4 Different Dimensions of Media

Despite the fact that network analysis has been integrated into the domain of communication research (Rogers and Kincaid 1981), the focus on personal networks two decades before shed more light on the topic. Students engage in a wide variety of different personal communication media, as described in the previous section, such as social networking sites, mobile communication through landlines or mobiles, or even platforms like Skype. Sociologists and media scientists have proposed several different ways of categorising the different media dimensions.

The habitual and conventional way of distinguishing media in terms of dissemination of information was old and new media, where old media consists of newspapers and hoardings, and new media encompasses electronic media like television and radio. When it comes to personal communication, the usual distinction is that made between the pre- and post-internet period. Phone calls and meeting someone fall under traditional media; using Facebook or calling a friend using a smartphone app are considered to be new media. The motive behind using a particular medium is related more or less to the social affordances of that medium.

With the diffusion of different technologies and the increase of new apps for smartphones, media convergence is playing a vital role in every person's life. The number of persons communicated with at once has also found its way into differentiating media: one-to-one, one-to-many, or many-to-many. Even though each media can be differentiated according to this division, it would be remiss to classify making phone calls into just one type—one-to-one—as phone calls can also be made to many people simultaneously through conference calls.

In empirical studies, there has been no clear unanimity on the underlying factor structure of different media used. Although social media data are analysed using factor analysis in market research to determine consumer quality and perception, the purpose of these sites from a social perspective is rarely focused on. In their study on the uses and gratifications of social media, Quan-Haase and Young (2010) compared the gratifications derived by using Facebook and IM, and found that Facebook was used more for fun and to be socially updated about others, while IM was used for relationship maintenance.

In order to identify independent media dimensions and reduce the complex structure of students' media use and frequency, I perform an explanatory factor analysis.[3] This method allows the variability among various media dimensions in terms of a potentially lower number of so-called factors to be studied. The variables measuring the type and frequency of media are reduced to underlying linear factors or components which are statistical entities having substantive meaning. That is, an international student might use Skype every day with their partner abroad, maintaining a long-term relationship, and might tend to meet in person twice a year as well. The different variables of media such as face-to-face interaction and video platforms according to their frequency having affinity to each other, are grouped together to produce different factors that are much more compliant.

The Three Media Profiles

Three distinct factors underpinned international student responses to the eight different media[4] dimensions employed in the study (type of media used and the frequency of use), and these factors were fairly consistent. The media dimensions of face-to-face interaction, phone calls, and text had factor loadings above 0.5, 0.5, and 0.6 respectively on Factor 1. I define this factor as the *classic media* as it is a quintessential model of personal communication. During the process, letters as a variable was eliminated as it did not contribute to a simple factor structure, failing to meet a minimum criterion of having a primary factor loading of 0.4 or above. The media dimensions of instant messaging and social networking sites loaded onto the second factor with a factor loading of 0.5 and 0.8 respectively (Table 3.2). This is called *neoteric media*, as it is novel as well as popular among the target group studied. The primary factor loadings are displayed in bold in Table 3.2.

Email had a factor loading of 0.4 and other platforms had a factor loading of 0.6, and both of them load onto the third factor which I call *established media*. The establishment of other tools like email was a complete changeover from the so-called traditional media use period, which was more or less phone and face-to-face interaction. Although different media have emerged, it is apparent that certain people adhere to certain media tools usage but that has set a trend where media like Skype, which

Table 3.2 Factor loadings based on a principal components analysis with varimax rotation for eight media dimensions (n = 1444)

	Classic media	Neoteric media	Established media
	Factor I	Factor II	Factor III
Text	**0.691**	0.218	0.166
Phone calls	**0.599**	0.168	0.297
Face to face	**0.566**	0.042	−0.24
Social networking	0.118	**0.824**	−0.044
Instant messaging	0.197	**0.579**	0.196
Other platforms	−0.096	0.367	**0.653**
Emails	0.302	−0.021	**0.41**
Letters	0.018	0.004	0.275
Eigenvalue	1.311	1.225	0.885
Per cent of variance	16.393	15.324	11.058

Note: Factor loadings < 0.3 are suppressed

uses video chat and email, have established themselves and reserved a place for themselves in the evolving process of media. It depends on the individual which medium they use to tactically meet their needs.

Notes

1. Source: Internet Live Stats (www.InternetLiveStats.com) April 1, 2018 Estimate. According to the International Telecommunications Union (ITU), an internet user is an individual (regardless of age) who can access the internet at home via any device type and connection.
2. Maslow's (1943) hierarchy of needs is a psychological theory illustrating the phases of growth such as physiological needs, safety, belongingness and love, esteem, self-actualisation, and self-transcendence in human beings.
3. Principal components analysis was employed because the main objective was to recognise and compute composite scores for the factors underlying the media dimensions.
4. Face-to-face contact, letters, text/SMS, phone calls, email, IM, social networking sites, and other platforms on a frequency scale, ranging from 0 = *Never*, 1 = *Less than five times a year*, 2 = *Five times a year*, 3 = *Several times a month*, 4 = *Once a month*, 5 = *Several times a month*, 6 = *Once a week*, 7 = *Several times a week*, 8 = *Daily*.

References

Ball-Rokeach, S. J., & DeFleur, M. L. (1976). A dependency model of mass-media effects. *Communication Research, 3*(1), 3–21.

Baym, N. K. (1998). The emergence of on-line community. *cybersociety, 2*(0), 35–68.

Bessiere, K., Kiesler, S., Kraut, R., & Boneva, B. S. (2008). Effects of Internet use and social resources on changes in depression. *Information, Community & Society, 11*(1), 47–70.

Boase, J. (2008). Personal networks and the personal communication system: Using multiple media to connect. *Information, Communication & Society, 11*(4), 490–508.

Castells, M. (2000). Toward a sociology of the network society. *Contemporary Sociology, 29*(5), 693–699.

Chen, W. (2010). Internet-usage patterns of immigrants in the process of intercultural adaptation. *Cyberpsychology, Behavior, and Social Networking, 13*(4), 387–399.

Costa, R. D. (2006). On a new concept of community: Social networks, personal communities and collective intelligence. *Interface-Comunicação, Saúde, Educação, 2*(SE), 0–0.

Daft, R. L., & Lengel, R. H. (1986). Organizational information requirements, media richness and structural design. *Management Science, 32*(5), 554–571.

Flanagin, A. J., & Metzger, M. J. (2001). Internet use in the contemporary media environment. *Human Communication Research, 27*(1), 153–181.

Fong, E., Wellman, B., Kew, M., & Wilkes, R. (2001). *Correlates of the digital divide: Individual, household and spatial variation*. Ottawa, Canada: Office of Learning Technologies, Human Resources Development.

Giddens, A. (1990). Structuration theory and sociological analysis. In J. Clark, C. Mogdil, & F. Mogdil (Eds.), *Anthony Giddens: Consensus and controversy* (pp. 297–315). Brighton: Falmer.

Gruzd, A., & Haythornthwaite, C. (2013). Enabling community through social media. *Journal of Medical Internet Research, 15*(10).

Haythornthwaite, C. (2000). Online personal networks: Size, composition and media use among distance learners. *New Media & Society, 2*(2), 195–226.

Haythornthwaite, C. (2005). Social networks and Internet connectivity effects. *Information, Community & Society, 8*(2), 125–147.

Hiller, H. H., & Franz, T. M. (2004). New ties, old ties and lost ties: The use of the internet in diaspora. *New Media & Society, 6*(6), 731–752.

Hogan, B. (2003). *Media multiplexity: An examination of differential communication usage*. Annual meeting of the Association of Internet Researchers, Toronto, Canada.

Hogan, B. J. (2009). *Networking in everyday life*. Toronto, ON, Canada: University of Toronto.

Jamieson, L. (2013). Personal relationships, intimacy and the self in a mediated and global digital age. In K. Orton-Johnson & N. Prior (Eds.), *Digital sociology* (pp. 13–33). London: Palgrave Macmillan.

Jenkins, H. (2006). *Convergence culture: Where old and new media collide*. New York University Press.

Katz, E. (1959). Mass communications research and the study of popular culture: An editorial note on a possible future for this journal. *Departmental Papers (ASC)*, 165.

Koku, E., Nazer, N., & Wellman, B. (2001). Netting scholars: Online and offline. *American Behavioral Scientist, 44*(10), 1752–1774.

Madianou, M., & Miller, D. (2013). *Migration and new media: Transnational families and polymedia*. Routledge.
Markus, M. L. (1994). Finding a happy medium: Explaining the negative effects of electronic communication on social life at work. *ACM Transactions on Information Systems (TOIS), 12*(2), 119–149.
Maslow, A. H. (1943). A theory of human motivation. *Psychological Review, 50*(4), 370–396.
McLuhan, M., & Fiore, Q. (1967). The medium is the message. *New York, 123*, 126–128.
Michelson, W. (2005). *Time use: Expanding explanation in the social sciences*. Boulder: Paradigm Publishers.
Mok, D., & Wellman, B. (2007). Did distance matter before the Internet?: Interpersonal contact and support in the 1970s. *Social Networks, 29*(3), 430–461.
Monge, P. R., & Contractor, N. S. (2001). Emergence of communication networks. In F. M. Jablin & L. L. Putnam (Eds.), *The new handbook of organizational communication: Advances in theory, research, and methods* (pp. 440–502). Thousand Oaks, CA: Sage.
Quan-Haase, A., & Young, A. L. (2010). Uses and gratifications of social media: A comparison of Facebook and instant messaging. *Bulletin of Science, Technology & Society, 30*(5), 350–361.
Quan-Haase, A., Wellman, B., Witte, J. C., & Hampton, K. N. (2002). Capitalizing on the net: Social contact, civic engagement, and sense of community. In B. Wellman & C. Haythornthwaite (Eds.), *The Internet in everyday life* (pp. 291–324). Oxford: Blackwell.
Rainie, L. (2006). Digital natives invade the workplace. In *Pew Internet & American life project: Washington, DC* (pp. 290–315).
Rainie, L., & Wellman, B. (2012). *Networked: The new social operating system*. MIT Press.
Reid, E. M. (1994). *Cultural formations in text-based virtual realities*. University of Melbourne.
Rheingold, H. (1985). *Tools for thought: The history and future of mind-expanding technology*. MIT Press.
Rheingold, H. (2000). *The virtual community: Homesteading on the electronic frontier*. MIT Press.
Rogers, E. M., & Kincaid, D. L. (1981). *Communication networks: Toward a new paradigm for research*. New York: Free Press.
Short, J., Williams, E., & Christie, B. (1976). *The social psychology of telecommunications*. Wiley.

Tu, C. H. (2002). The measurement of social presence in an online learning environment. *International Journal on E-Learning, 1*(2), 34–45.

Tu, C. H., & McIsaac, M. (2002). The relationship of social presence and interaction in online classes. *The American Journal of Distance Education, 16*(3), 131–150.

Turkle, S. (2011). *Alone together: Why we expect more from technology and less from ourselves*. New York: Basic Books.

Veenhof, B., Wellman, B., Quell, C., & Hogan, B. (2008). *How Canadians' use of the Internet affects social life and civic participation*. Ottawa: Statistics Canada.

Wellman, B. (2001). Little boxes, glocalization, and networked individualism. In *Kyoto Workshop on Digital Cities* (pp. 10–25). Berlin, Heidelberg: Springer.

Wellman, B., & Haythornthwaite, C. (Eds.). (2008). *The Internet in everyday life*. John Wiley & Sons.

Wellman, B., Hogan, B., Berg, K., Boase, J., Carrasco, J.-A., Côté, R., Kayahara, J., Kennedy, T. L., & Tran, P. (2006). Connected lives: The project. In P. Purcell (Ed.), *Networked neighbourhoods* (pp. 161–216). Springer.

Wellman, B., Quan-Haase, A., Boase, J., & Chen, W. (2002). Examining the Internet in everyday life. In *Keynote address to the Euricom Conference on e-Democracy, Nijmegen, Netherlands (October).*

Wellman, B., & Wortley, S. (1990). Different strokes from different folks: Community ties and social support. *American Journal of Sociology, 96*(3), 558–588.

Zerubavel, E. (1982). The standardization of time: A sociohistorical perspective. *American Journal of Sociology, 88*(1), 1–23.

4

Network Constituents: Exploring Contents

4.1 International Student Mobility

In an intercultural communication class, I noticed that the most memorable experience for almost everyone was the time spent studying abroad. It might be an eye-opener for some, exciting or unforgettable for another person, but nothing less than interesting any time. Studying in a city, or country in the case of international students, away from family or friends is a very different but at the same time invigorating experience. People move in and out of the network, but this might very well be dependent on the duration as well. Whatever happens, there will be a distinctive set of people, very different from the countless ones that one passes daily, ensuring that they are present in the network. The new milieu poses a challenge at the beginning and then, after the initial academic adjustment, they acquire knowledge of the local settings and are more aware of the nuances of higher education.

International student mobility has always been part of higher education, but in different ways that have wide-ranging aspects. The space within which international student mobility now takes place has become a transnational one, characterised by multiple ties and interactions linking people and institutions across the borders of nation states (Rizvi 2005).

R. Kanagavel, *The Social Lives of Networked Students*,
https://doi.org/10.1007/978-3-319-96199-6_4

Considering that, I would like to contend that modern-day transnational formations have a considerable influence upon international student mobility. In line with Rizvi, Steffan Mau (2010)—when addressing student mobility in Germany—claims that there is a profound effect of transnationalisation on students in terms of social transnationalism such as their maintenance of social relationships across borders in everyday life. The postulation that the change from home to host culture is a goal-oriented process is also challenging. The transition stage brings the question of whether they receive and provide support in a complex yet unpretentious environment. Students will make their own choices as to whom to contact, and from whom to seek and to whom to deliver support.

Specifically, I deal with ego-centred networks, with international students being the egos. The students not only come across and identify the transnational activities but also actively participate. The pattern of relationships within a network makes up the structural variables like network density, centrality, or isolation. These are in contrast to compositional variables that summarise the characteristics of alters within the personal network, such as the number of female members, the average age, or the average intensity of the relationship.

4.2 Characteristics of Personal Networks

After discussing the international students at the individual level and their network members at the relational level, I inspect the contents and processes taking place in these networks. Contrary to the general notion of a community being fixed in a particular location, they tend to maintain their own personal communities by travelling to make in-person visits, and phoning to maintain contact between these visits.

Relationships can be abiding or transitory. The transitory nature of relationships is even more evident among relationships that are not very strong. This can be well-explained through an example of an international student who was cultural secretary at his university in his home country a year ago. During that time, due to the size of the university, more than 50 people worked for the cultural programme under his leadership but the friendship with these students from different faculties eventually faded over the course of time, after he moved away for higher studies. Above all, it can be said that people will often form many sets of relationships throughout their lives, especially with career changes and movement to different places. The maintenance of ties depends on the student's networking pattern, and at the same time the constitution of ties. I discuss the composition and structure of personal networks, considering the information on the characteristics of social contacts and the pattern of relationships.

Structural Properties

One postulation behind network research is that structured social relationships bring forth more meaningful explanations than individualistic characteristics in a social network. This basically reinforces the fact that more than the presence of relationships, it is the pattern of relationships that gives an explanation for the social phenomena taking place (Brass 1995). I introduce primary structural aspects to provide a first impression of the networks of the international students surveyed.

The number of networks corresponds to the number of people who participated in the survey. The average mean of the network size of the international students' networks ($N = 287$) is 7.04 (SD = 4.54). This is similar to the online study conducted by Manfreda et al. (2004) which obtained an average network size of 7.5 with the help of a four-item name generator. The network size is positively skewed, ranging from one to 27 members. There are 13 egocentric networks, which have a size of one. A significant number of networks (13 per cent) have four alters and nearly 25 per cent mentioned eight alters in their networks (Fig. 4.1). Regarding the emotional intensity of the ties in the network, it can be seen that there are 30–40 per cent very close ties in smaller networks, with alters ranging from two to five.

The distribution of network size corresponds to other studies with similar questionnaires. As nearly 50 international students (21.4 per cent) reported more than eight alters in their network, random selection was made to choose the subsample for which name interpreters were

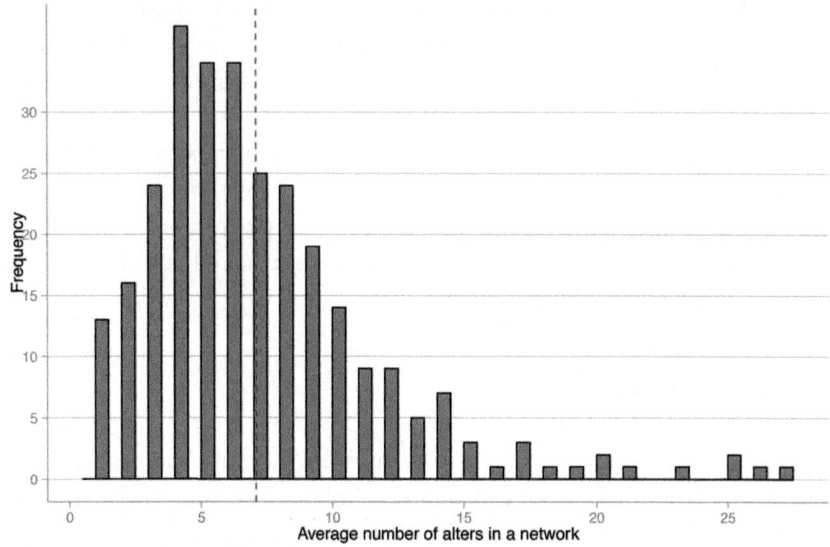

Fig. 4.1 Network size (*N* = 287)

directed. Out of the total of 2023 alters, 389 alters who were supportive were trimmed off in the subsample, and those relationships were used only for information on support rather than the other content. The number elicited in the study might also depend on the instrument, for example on role relationships, closeness factors, or support. The closeness approach used by Wellman's team primarily delineated the strong and active ties, ruling out acquaintances and distant friends in terms of relational intensity.

To study the different types of network, the size can be related to social categories to give an overall idea. The comparison of averages in size of the networks on the basis of gender shows that the networks of women and men vary in size. The average size of male networks is 5.78 (*N* = 84) and of female networks is 7.38 (*N* = 158). Heavy communicators are supposed to have larger and more diverse personal networks. By comparing the size with the number of internet hours spent, the size reaches a threshold of eight hours for a network with eight alters. After this point, as the size increases, it can be seen that the hours spent on the internet reduce, with few outliers.

The density of the networks represents the internal interconnections of the individual ego-centred networks. This is calculated through alter-alter relationships, which were surveyed for eight alters. The density is calculated only for networks with at least two alters. Only 229 networks out of the total of 287 were considered, and the mean network density is 0.47. There is much variation in the structure of the networks and this can be described quantitatively. The structural aspects of personal community size (number of alters) and density negatively correlated moderately with each other ($r = -0.489$, $p < 0.000$). The negative trend shows that with an increase in the size of the network, its density decreases. People in larger networks know each other to a lesser extent. In nearly four per cent of the personal networks none of the mentioned alters know each other, whereas all of the members of the network know each other in 13 per cent. There is a positive correlation between density and degree (number of existing ties) at $r = 0.28$, $p < 0.000$. As number of alters increases linearly, the number of possible ties increases geometrically (since density is a function of the number of alters), so it becomes less likely that the number of actual ties will stay proportionate to the number of alters.

Compositional Characteristics

Coming to the networks' member age, the average age of an alter per network was found to be 30.03 (SD = 8.72). The network size is compared in terms of the age of the international students in relation to the transnational ties. When the relationship between network size and age was examined, it was found to be directly proportional: as the age of the students increases, there is an increase in the size of the networks. Younger international students tend to have smaller networks than older students. Around 67 per cent of the networks are made up of people whose age is less than 30 (Table 4.1). This ratifies the statement that age homogeneity is generally high when people are young, as friends are made at that age (Allan 1989).

The strength of the relationships, which may be strong or weak, matters in every single network. Although it is expected that the elicitation procedure will impart supportive relationships that tend to be close, it

Table 4.1 Characteristics of personal networks ($n = 2023$ $N = 287$)

	Per cent
Female	55.2
Age	
Young (<30)	66.7
Middle (30–60)	30.2
Old (>60)	3
Role relationships	
Spouse	9.7
Family	20.2
Friends	43.2
Vicinity	14.6
Others	0.2
Emotional intensity	
Very close	46.4
Close	26.2
Somewhat close	19.3
Less close	5.7
Not close	2.3
Duration	
Known <1	25.9
Known 1 > 10 years	41.5
Known >10 years	29.4

would be interesting to sneak a view of the constitution with respect to strength. Nearly half of the networks (46.4 per cent) are occupied by strong ties as anticipated, and the categories of close and somewhat close ties make up around 26 and 19 per cent of the networks respectively. Only around two per cent were not close at all, and these ties are accounted for by rare role relationships. The role played by the relationships tends to be more or less the same whereas the ties can be flexible, so that there is a constant change in the network. There is a prevalence of friend (43 per cent) relationships in the networks, while spouse and family make up around 10 and 20 per cent respectively. Few relationships emerge from being in the same setting or area, be it classroom or neighbourhood. I call such relationships vicinity ties and they represent around 14.6 per cent, comprising classmates, flatmates, and neighbours. While interrelating role relationships by emotional intensity, I found that friends, parents, and spouses are the highest among the strong (very close) ties whereas colleagues and classmates are highest under close ties.

Early sociologists (Simmel 2012; Coser 2017) accentuated the concept of homophily by claiming that associating with people from different social backgrounds has become essential to life in modern societies. This can be applied to students, who have become even more networked due to digital technologies when maintaining their personal communities. International students develop rich sources and intricate sets of roles with people. This is usually done through casual conversations and interactions with people from these different backgrounds. They are in fact interchanging and swapping between different social networks, retrieving new ideas and information that are mutual to those groups.

Looking at the homophily exhibited by the international students through Putnam's dichotomy of social capital (bonding and bridging),[1] nearly half of them are implicit affinities and explicit connections, in terms of characteristics like social location, age, and gender. In other words, they mingle and share a bond with a person having characteristics similar to theirs: in Putnam's words this is referred to as having potential for bonding capital as well as connecting to each other explicitly. In the study, it was found that the students had their peers or people of the same age in an average of 15 per cent of their networks. This proportion escalated to 53 per cent when the age group of three years younger or older than the student was considered instead of the same age group.

On average, students had 64 per cent of ties from the same country of residence and 58 per cent of ties from the same country of origin. Although some individuals had only people from the same country of residence (29 per cent) and same country of origin (24 per cent) in their networks, others did take the opportunity to go beyond the implicit affinities. The students had nearly 60 per cent of their ties of the same gender on average in their networks.

4.3 Disentangling the 'Trans'

The personal networks of the surveyed international students are described using key dimensions, focusing the analysis in the context of transnational perspectives and viewing it together with other characteristics of the networks. The following questions lead the descriptive analysis, bringing forth the intricacy of personal communities and the importance of transnationalism: How strong and big are the personal networks dominated by transnational relations? What is the proportion of transnational relations in the network, and how are the transnational relations embedded structurally within the networks? With whom are they connected transnationally? How do transnational and non-transnational relationships differ with regard to support received and given? Does this also affect the number of support dimensions? How are they in contact (which medium and with what frequency)? How is this interrupted by role relationships? Are there different constellations in terms of media and support in the observed relationships?

The differences in the transnationality of the personal networks can be explained by mobility patterns and also the duration of stay of the students in their current country of residence. The combined reflection of migration and specific personal characteristics and transnational approaches in personal networks will make this more rational. Before that, it is also beneficial to take a closer look at the proportions within the two broad categories of transnationality: transnational and non-transnational ties. The transnationality of a network member (coded as 0 = non-transnational, 1 = transnational) in a network is aggregated to the network level to show the proportion of transnational ties.

Only-transnational ties constitute 8.7 per cent of the international students' networks, whereas 25.1 per cent of the networks do not have any transnational ties. The distribution of the proportion of transnational relationships depicts that transnationality in the form of transnational relations does not fall under the category of networks, either comprising only-transnational ties or no transnational ties. The categorisations are thus made accordingly so that there are other classifications apart from these two distinct categories. The average number of transnational relations (33–67 per cent) is the most highly represented (n = 109) among the international students. After all, 74.8 per cent of students maintain at least one transnational relationship, with nearly a tenth of the observed personal networks consisting entirely of alters living outside their current country of residence.

Extending "Transnational" to "Local"

A large proportion of the ties live in another country (36.5 per cent) which represents transnational ties. Within the same country, relationships of all categories are represented together as one category, non-transnational ties, consisting of 73.5 per cent of the ties. This is further classified for more clarity according to the specific geographical location. Molina et al. (2012) examined the geographical dispersion of personal networks of native-born and foreign-born residents living in Catalonia and found that native-born people had more local contacts and foreign-born residents indicated a degree of transnationalism. Herz (2015) while studying German migrants in Great Britain, reports that the networks of the migrants, even though they had transnational contacts, were bound within Europe. This finding reflects that they are organised in a few specific regions 'translocally'. This is quite opposite to the phenomenon of glocalisation (Hampton and Wellman 2002) in an even broader space of how most social relationships were built with people living within a small distance and having very few people who are living in different parts of the world. On average, 54.7 per cent of the networks consist of intra-continental ties and the rest (45.3 per cent) have all ties on the same continent, that is, intercontinental ties, thus painting a picture that combines both aspects of translocalisation and glocalisation.

Transnational Embeddedness

Based on the average personal network with seven network members (SD = 4.54) the alters for the 287 students correspond to a nearly 40 per cent share in transnational relationships (M = 0.37, SD = 0.31). There is a weak relationship between the proportion of transnational relations and the number of alters per network (network size) where changes are not correlated ($r = 0.026$, $p = 0.655$). And there is a negative correlation between the proportion of transnational relations and the density of a personal network ($r = -0.078$, $p = 0.237$). This means that an increasing proportion of transnational relations is associated with a lower affinity of

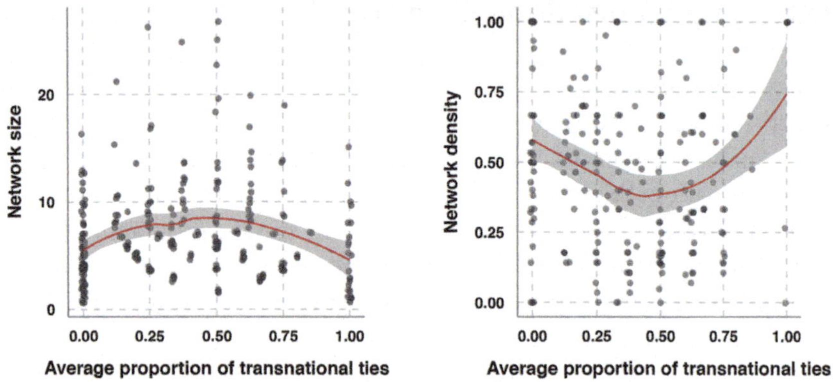

Fig. 4.2 Transnationality vs. density and transnationality vs. size

the personal networks. It is apparent that transnationality in terms of the proportion of transnational relations is independent of size and dependent on density (Fig. 4.2). It is clear that the personal networks of the international students surveyed can be considered to be part of the transnational phenomenon.

Configuration of a Transnational Network

Although the categorisation of ties is boundary bound, network members are not restricted to borders and include people who have moved but still remain part of the network of the students. This means that they also comprise peers as well as friends in the current country of residence irrespective of their nationality. In order to get an idea of the social life of the international students and their integration with other students, questions on being a member of any association/group (not necessarily based in your present country of residence) whose members are mainly of your origin, as well as any association/group whose members are mainly international students, were asked. It is observed that 37 per cent of the students were involved in activities in organisations whose members are primarily of their origin and 45 per cent in organisations whose members are mainly international students.

A functional model was developed by Bochner and his team (1977) to study friendship patterns of students who were enrolled in universities outside their home countries and thus classified as overseas students. It was the first of its kind and comprised three types of network: A co-national network, a network with host nationals, and a multi-national network (Bochner et al. 1977). In a study on international doctoral students in Germany (Bilecen 2014), friendship networks are segregated into co-German (co-national international friends in Germany), int-German (international friends in Germany), co-abroad (co-national international friends abroad), and int-abroad (international friends abroad) networks. While the aforementioned studies have used this categorisation mainly to analyse cross-cultural friendships, Brandes et al. (2010) distinguish four types of social contacts by blending national and geographical categories to study migrants. Following this categorisation, I will describe the international students' networks. The *origin* accounts for nearly half of the students' networks on average, conveying that 50 per cent of the alters are the co-nationals of the student who are living in the home country. The co-national contacts who live in the host country are termed *fellow* and make up about 27 per cent of the networks. While the *host* category (natives of the host country) constitute around 30 per cent of the networks of the international students, all other alters from a third nationality or living in a third country known as *transnational* represent 31 per cent.

For the international students interviewed for the study it is shown that both the number of shorter stays (less than three months) outside the current country of residence in general ($r = 0.070$, $p < 0.001$) and the second longest stay abroad ($r = 0.066$, $p < 0.001$) have a very low linear correlation with the proportion of transnational relations. This connection, albeit small, makes it clear that people who are often transnationally mobile have a higher proportion of transnational relations.

Relating Transnationality to Students' Characteristics

The proportion of transnational ties seems to increase along with age at the youngest ages, but in the end, for the age group 31 and above, there is a decrease in the proportion of transnational ties (Fig. 4.3). Communities

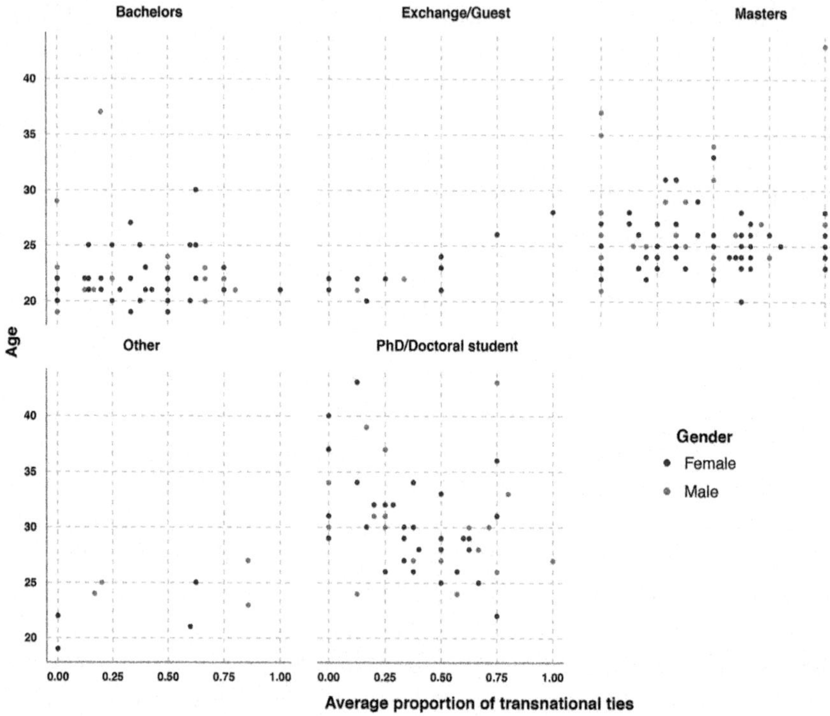

Fig. 4.3 Characteristics of the students by the proportion of transnational ties

with higher education are characterised by a larger transnational expansion (Dahinden 2009). It is assumed that students with higher education tend to have more transnational ties. Although it is partially true in the sample, the scenario is completely different in the context of international students. Both master's and PhD students have higher proportions of transnational ties (both exhibiting 39 per cent) than students enrolled in bachelor's and exchange programmes (34 per cent). At the same time, students pursuing other programmes like diploma courses tend to have the highest number of transnational ties. This might be due to the short duration of the stay in the current country of residence where not many local ties are made.

Closeness and Role by Geographical Distance

The emotional significance of the relationships was discussed in the descriptive section and it was found that there was a high number of very close ties. Can this be explained through network characteristics of transnationality? Fischer (1982) states that distant associates are notably more likely to be close than others. To be close with someone geographically is different, as it is not linearly related to the emotional intensity of relationships.

The mean values of relationship socio-emotional intensity for each geographical distance class shows that the majority of the very close ties are more likely to live in another country, and the second highest live in the same household or in the same city. Within the geographical regions, transnational (63 per cent), local (43 per cent), and household (42 per cent) ties are very close, whereas national and regional ties are not close (see Fig. 4.4). It was found that cross-border relations in particular have high relationship intensity.

Despite the large geographical distance, it is found that transnational relations have a strong emotional bond. This interesting finding can be related to the maintained contact which is discussed later in the section. The level of emotional intensity, which is measured by the closeness in the transnational relationships, raises the question of to whom those ties belong. The transnational relations which largely consist of ties belonging to the home country are also more likely to be family and friends, where it can be assumed that the emotional intensity of the relationship is high. This raises the interesting question of whether cross-border relationships can be maintained as a great emotional bond. This will be dealt when analysing the frequency of contact of the relationships. Apart from that, how can personal networks be differentiated in the context of role relationships?

When relating transnationality to role relationships, it is noticeable that transnational ties belonging to family members—such as parents (28 per cent), relatives (5 per cent), and siblings (15 per cent)—outnumber the non-transnational ties in this category. Although there is a predominance of friends (46 per cent) in transnational relationships, it is

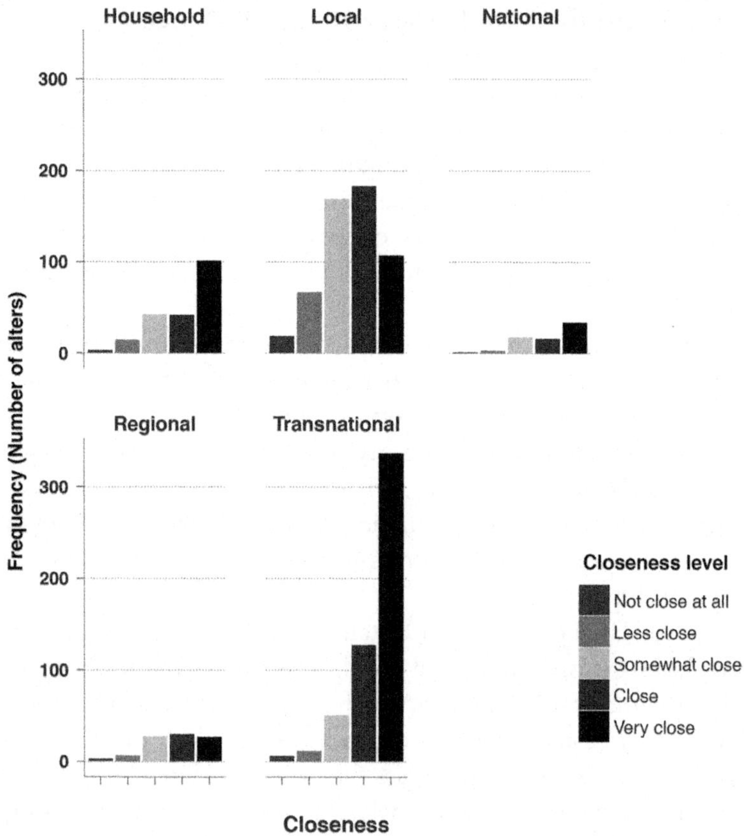

Fig. 4.4 Closeness by geographical distance

relatively low when compared to the non-transnational ties who are friends. As predicted, transnational relationships belong mainly to friends and family, especially intimate family members like parents and siblings. Under the non-transnational ties, household ties consist mainly of spouse/partners (23 per cent) and flatmates (43 per cent), and colleagues and friends are the highest amongst other non-transnational categories. How are these far-flung as well as nearby ties—which are full of resources in the form of various role relationships—contacted?

Mediation of Transnational Connections

With the advent of the internet there is indeed a sharp rise in transnational relationships, which can be local as well as geographically dispersed. There is a subtle straightforwardness between the maintenance of long-distance relationships and the widespread use of the internet. As many scholars have already discussed, internet communication is not limited by physical limitations. It is possible to communicate with anyone who has access to a computer and internet connection, anywhere in the world. In the Netville project (2006), which took place in Toronto, it was found that the internet was used to maintain both local and non-local relationships (Fig. 4.5).

Although many relationships are often formed with people who have mutual friends, the internet also affords the formation of relationships between those who do not share common social relationships. The transitory nature of relationships implies that social relationships are not only being disorientated, they are also being moulded. The internet definitely serves as a means both to form new relationships and to enhance existing relationships. For example, Hampton and Wellman (2002) find that people moving to a different locality use the internet to maintain ties with former neighbours. There are a few affordances offered, which is more advantageous when having to deal with people face-to-face on a personal level. Nowadays, with media convergence, there is a shift in the paradigm from one-to-one person interactivity to one-to-many persons interactivity. Although online forums are not predominantly a common way to meet new people, they nonetheless provide assistance for those who might have issues forming relationships.

Contacts can be mediated through communication media, when cross-border news is discussed over the phone, Skype, or mail (Vertovec 2009). Latané et al. (1995) and Mok et al. (2010) point out that geographical distance is inversely proportional to frequency of contact. It can be assumed that as geographical distance increases between the students and their network members, there is a decrease in frequency of contact, and transnational relationships are rarely activated. This raises a question of whether contacts as a function of ego are constructed differently

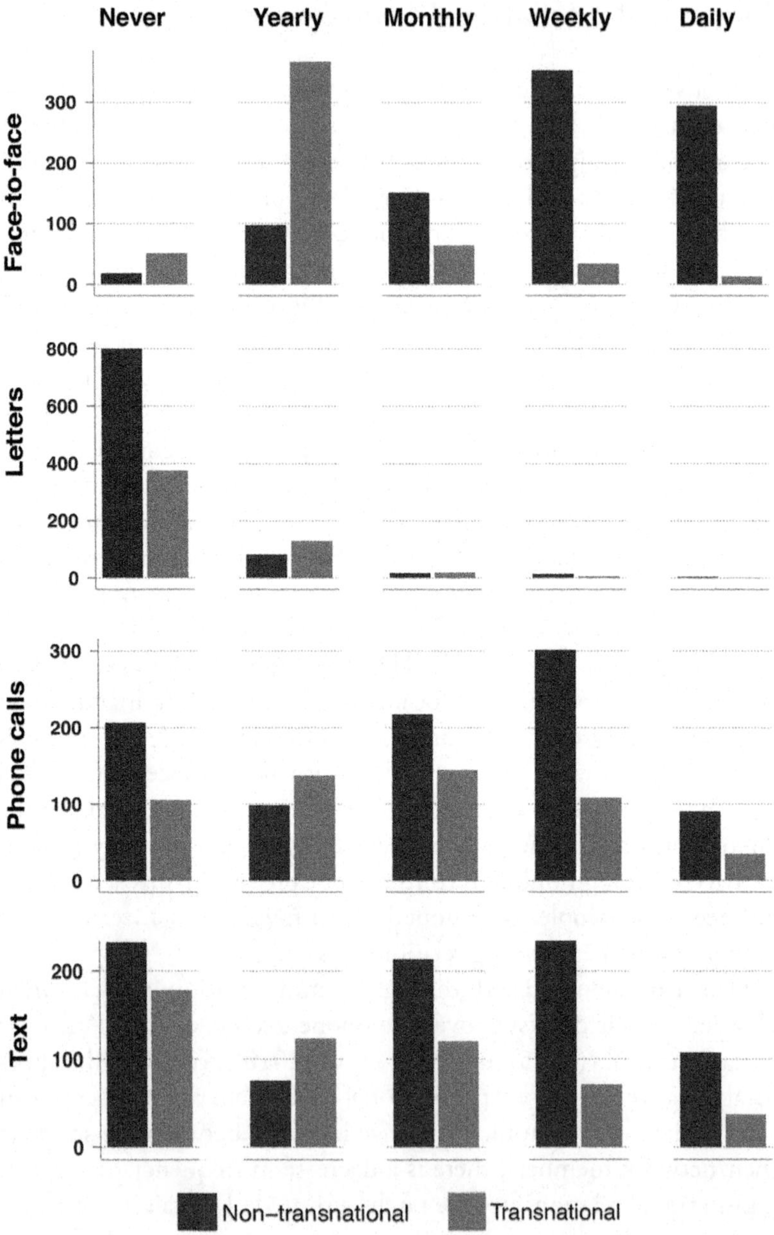
Never
Yearly
Monthly
Weekly
Daily
Face-to-face
Letters
Phone calls
Text
300
200
100
0
800
600
400
200
0
300
200
100
0
200
100
0
Non–transnational
Transnational

(continued)

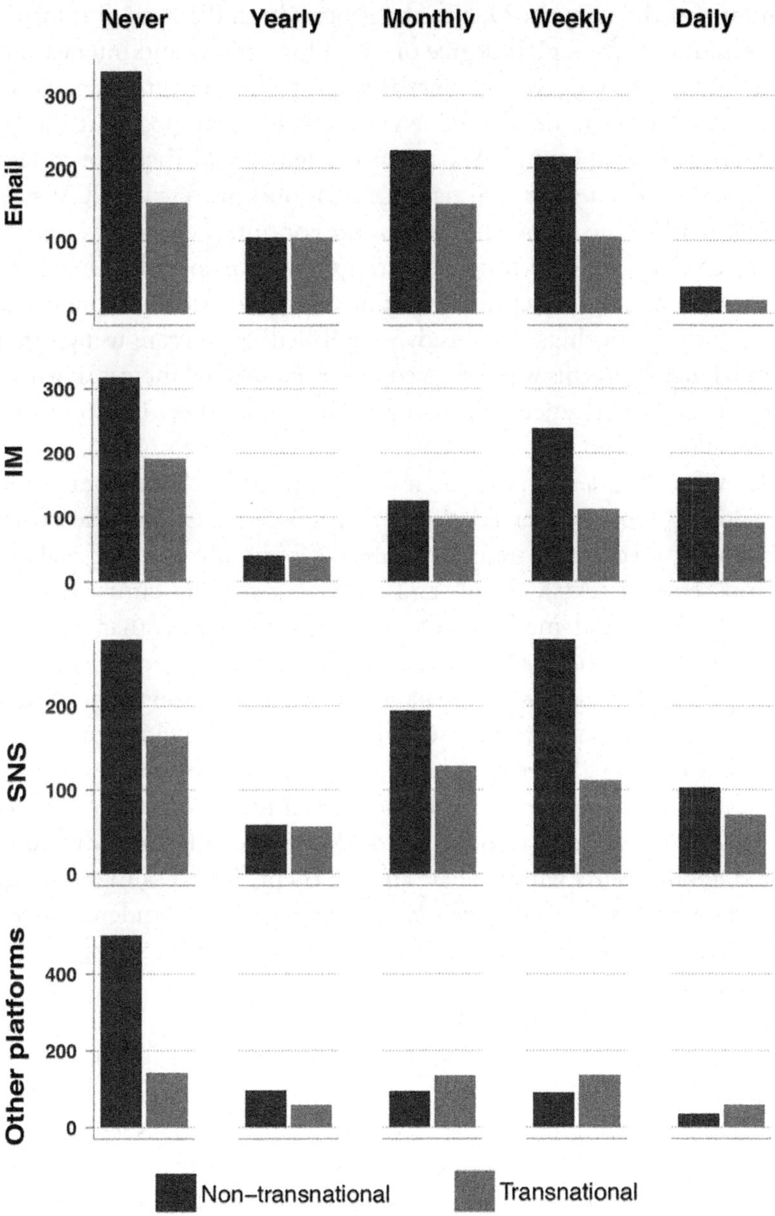

Fig. 4.5 Type of media channel used according to frequency by transnationality

depending on the context. Due to the geographical distance of transnational ties, they have a high degree of social formations and interactions (Portes 1999). How do you contact this particular person when physically abroad? Contacts are maintained not only by technology but also by face-to-face communication. So, it can be rightly said that face-to-face contact has a meaning for transnational relationships. Urry (2003) suggests that not just media are required for the continued existence of social relations contact, but face-to-face meetings play a major role. They hold a special place among other different kinds of media used for contact, as some of the relationships are already established well before using other additional media. In this way, the need to stay connected increases, which may not occur when a person is living nearby. This aspect is also related to physical relocation.

This raises the question of which communication channels are used for managing cross-border relations. Fig. 4.5 demonstrates the cross-tabulation of media and transnationality. Mobile phones (for making calls and sending texts), email, and social networking sites were the most frequently used media to connect with local ties, that is, non-transnational ties, whereas Instant Messenger and other social platforms like Skype dominate among transnational ties. Even though social networking sites help people who are dispersed across the globe to stay in touch, confronting the geographical factor, as per the pre-test, more local ties than transnational ties are contacted using social networking sites. One of the reasons accounting for this is that it keeps individuals updated about events which occur around them. It allows them to tap into their peripheral social network, thus widening the students' social life. Face-to-face contact is primarily local, which involves mainly short-distance relationships.

When talking about friendship networks, they can be easily maintained through online forums. Social networking sites like Facebook have various features and privacy settings where you can form groups from different contexts within your own social networks as well as with people who share mutual interests, and can also maintain your individual profile. With the mobile revolution taking place now—and students being the majority of the consumers—it is common to have a mobile with an internet connection (smartphone). With this technological advancement, tech-savvy people can connect to another person who is from the other side of the world via the small device in their hand. Despite these social affordances, research suggests that networked individuals are not totally submerged within the mobile revolution and that they prefer to see the members of their networks from time to time. In the early 2000s, email was considered to be an easy medium as it is asynchronous and provides an avenue for easier communication with people from diverse social backgrounds. Nowadays, however, international students primarily use email with people in formal settings such as professor or work colleagues. The media channels, used to communicate with varied social ties, are chosen according to the role relationship and the networking pattern of the network members.

The diverse social ties are largely categorised in the literature of social networks as weak and strong ties. There are at least two simple ways that online communication helps or affords the maintenance of weak and strong ties. Firstly, it helps people to organise meetings more suitably than does the phone. The asynchronous nature of these media helps or gives a chance to communicate with weak ties in a way that is not intrusive. Dunbar (2010) revealed that a person can maintain only 150 relationships in a society or even on Facebook. So, when a person has more than 500 or 1000 friends on Facebook, it is merely their own extension of their social networks, which consists mostly of weak ties. These ties can be acquaintances, people from a particular place or locality, or even people with whom they have had just one conversation. This explains the second advantage of using this kind of communication to maintain these kinds of weak relationships, and also how it can be helpful in certain situations. For example, a person who is an expert from a particular field whom you met once a long time ago can provide you with information on the job market, which could not be provided by a close friend with whom you share a stronger relationship.

The various aspects of transnationality have been studied up until now, and it has been shown that networks of students have a high degree of geographic and spatial expansion. However, this spatial distribution of personal networks points to the central question of provision of support. Several studies have demonstrated the importance of social support from people living far away, despite the geographical dispersion (Herz 2015; Bilecen 2014; Mok and Wellman 2007; Mok et al. 2010; Wellman 1979). This somehow gives the idea that different forms of social support are dependent on geographical distance. I examine this by interrelating the support dimensions with the aspect of transnationality (geographical distance of the alters).

Personal matters are shared predominantly with people living abroad (43.5 per cent) followed by people living in the same city as the student (33.7 per cent). Along with the household ties, the local ties who provide emotional support make up 47 per cent. Students reciprocate support to the ties that provide support. At the same time, they also tend to provide help or support to others in the network. Kobayashi and Boase (2014) define reciprocity as "normative recognition", that if a person helps another person, they will receive help from others as well, creating positive influence and satisfaction. The emotional support reciprocated from the international student to their network members is almost the same as the emotional support received, with only a one per cent difference. Instrumental support is predominantly received from the local and household ties (41.7 per cent and 23.2 per cent) and given by the international student to the transnational ties (40.1 per cent). Information assistance is majorly sought from, and given back to, transnational ties (38.3 per cent and 43.3 per cent). Moving on to social companionship, it was observed that leisure time is mainly spent with local ties (49.6 per cent received and 39.3 per cent given).

Considering the impact of geographical and spatial distance on the relative frequency of social support, for individual types of support, is only one way of looking at the question of whether the use of social support is influenced by distance. The theoretical considerations suggest that there is an increasing transformation in the relationship due to the geographical distance between students and the members of their networks. In a similar way, this also happens to the range of mediated support content. I explore the support system, especially the property of support multiplexity in relation with other characteristics, in Chap. 5.

Note

1. Bonding refers to the tendency that individuals may have to associate with others who are similar to them, leading to homogeneous groups. Bridging occurs when individuals associate with others who are not like them, leading to heterogeneous groups (Putnam 2000; Putnam and Feldstein 2009).

References

Allan, G. (1989). *Friendship: Developing a sociological perspective.* Boulder, CO: Westview Press.

Bilecen, B. (2014). *International student mobility and transnational friendships.* New York: Palgrave Macmillan.

Bochner, S., McLeod, B. M., & Lin, A. (1977). Friendship patterns of overseas students: A functional model. *International Journal of Psychology, 12*(4), 277–294.

Brandes, U., Lerner, J., Lubbers, M. J., McCarty, C., Molina, J. L., & Nagel, U. (2010). Recognizing modes of acculturation in personal networks of migrants. *Procedia – Social and Behavioral Sciences, 4*, 4–13.

Brass, D. J. (1995). Creativity: It's all in your social network. In C. M. Ford & D. A. Gioia (Eds.), *Creative action in organizations* (pp. 94–99). Thousand Oaks, CA: Sage.

Coser, L. A. (2017). *The idea of social structure: Papers in honor of Robert K. Merton*. Routledge.

Dahinden, J. (2009). Are we all transnationals now? Network transnationalism and transnational subjectivity: The differing impacts of globalization on the inhabitants of a small Swiss city. *Ethnic and Racial Studies, 32*(8), 1365–1386.

Dunbar, R. (2010). *How many friends does one person need?: Dunbar's number and other evolutionary quirks*. Faber & Faber.

Fischer, C. S. (1982). *To dwell among friends: Personal networks in town and city.* University of Chicago Press.

Hampton, K., & Wellman, B. (2002). The not so global village of Netville. In B. Wellman & C. Haythornthwaite (Eds.), *The Internet in everyday life* (pp. 345–371). Oxford: Blackwell.

Herz, A. (2015). Relational constitution of social support in migrants' transnational personal communities. *Social Networks, 40*, 64–74.

Kobayashi, T., & Boase, J. (2014). Tele-cocooning: Mobile texting and social scope. *Journal of Computer-Mediated Communication, 19*(3), 681–694.
Latané, B., Liu, J. H., Nowak, A., Bonevento, M., & Zheng, L. (1995). Distance matters: Physical space and social impact. *Personality and Social Psychology Bulletin, 21*(8), 795–805.
Manfreda, K. L., Vehovar, V., & Hlebec, V. (2004). Collecting ego-centred network data via the Web. *Metodoloski zvezki, 1*(2), 295.
Mau, S. (2010). *Social transnationalism: Lifeworlds beyond the nation-state.* Routledge.
Mok, D., & Wellman, B. (2007). Did distance matter before the Internet?: Interpersonal contact and support in the 1970s. *Social Networks, 29*(3), 430–461.
Mok, D., Wellman, B., & Carrasco, J. (2010). Does distance matter in the age of the Internet? *Urban Studies, 47*(13), 2747–2783.
Molina, J. L., Lozares, C., & Lubbers, M. J. (2012). The geographical distribution of the personal networks of people living in Catalonia: A dual society. *GRAFO Working Papers, 1*, 1–19.
Portes, A. (1999). Conclusion: Towards a new world-the origins and effects of transnational activities. *Ethnic and Racial Studies, 22*(2), 463–477.
Putnam, R. D. (2000). *Bowling alone: The collapse and revival of American community.* New York: Simon and Schuster.
Putnam, R. D., & Feldstein, L. (2009). *Better together: Restoring the American community.* New York: Simon and Schuster.
Rizvi, F. (2005). Rethinking "brain drain" in the era of globalisation. *Asia Pacific Journal of Education, 25*(2), 175–192.
Simmel, G. (2012). The metropolis and mental life. In *The urban sociology reader* (pp. 37–45). Routledge.
Urry, J. (2003). *Global complexity.* Cambridge: Polity Press.
Vertovec, S. (2009). *Transnationalism.* Routledge.
Wellman, B. (1979). The community question: The intimate networks of East Yorkers. *American Journal of Sociology, 84*(5), 1201–1231.

5

Network Patterns: Combining Features

Using network compositional information, I have summarised and contextualised students' relationships. The information about the interconnection among their relationships allowed me to look at the dynamics of the networks. With this data, I explore different patterns in students' networks and examine how their connections thrive and how they communicate. To begin with, I will describe the different types of network patterns that emerged from the data. The typology and the presentation of the different patterns of the international students' networks is differentiated in terms of the use and frequency of media channels. I view the identified structure formations through the transnationality feature. After determining the network patterns, I examine the same constellations in relation to the demographic information of the students. In this way, it might be possible to check whether the patterns are centred on the differences in the network and relational features. Subsequently, the question is posed as to whether the different formation is a condition for the provision of social support.

International students have inherent features that reflect upon the persistent as well as pertinent approaches for networking. When it comes to media usage patterns, each individual has their preferences and their own style of networking in accordance with Wellman's concept of "networked

R. Kanagavel, *The Social Lives of Networked Students*,
https://doi.org/10.1007/978-3-319-96199-6_5

individualism". The spatial and temporal features have an influence on these patterns of networking but are definitely not fixed upon by them. Having said that, it can be interpreted that networking is a relational attribute of an individual, which they adapt and maintain. Despite the different network patterns identified, I recognise—and also acknowledge in the study—that students connect and operate within a network in a unique way in accordance with their communication flow as well as social behaviour. The variation of media use and frequency of an individual connecting with people in the network is measured through a *particularity* score (Hogan 2009). At the end of this chapter, I calculate this score, that is, the difference in media employed by the international students to connect with their network members, and also review the factors influencing the *particularity* score.

Students are at the centre of their personal networks. Structured social relationships are a potent fountainhead of sociological explanations than personal characteristics of the network members (Wellman 1988). In the study, the range of connections in students' networks is between one and 27. Following the establishment of a relationship between the student and their network members, the structural location has a great impact on the relationships as well as networks. Likewise, the framework of ties in a social system notably affects the flow of resources through specific ties, as illustrated by the example of Monica in the *Friends* TV series as the mother hen of the whole group. First, she was the one who introduced everyone in the group to each other and then, somehow, they end up being together until the end. Proximity may even play an important role when it comes to the activation of the latent ties. A classic example would be how Ross and Rachael end up together in *Friends*.

Structural analysts interpret all dyadic relations in the light of the aggregation and interconnectivity of links among network members. They point out that the dyadic relations can only be understood in the context of the structures formed by their linkages. This focus on structural form distinguishes structural analysis from other social approaches, such as exchange theory, which look primarily at relational patterns as they condition dyadic ties. Even social systems that do not involve people have structural properties that are more than the sum of dyadic exchanges. The structures of social relationships tend to have a greater explanatory power and are therefore articulated as individual characteristics (Freeman 2004). This idea suggests that structural features of personal communities in the specific context of international students are effective. It is better to look at social structure, and this is exactly why I study the students' networking patterns at the structural level.

The extensive effects of the social division and contents of ties make the Community Question (Wellman 1979) an important issue for many sociologists. Previous studies, which mainly concentrated on the classification of community, focused on the inherent notion that social activities are saved for the local neighbourhood, and this was a follow-up for further research activities. However, other important reference points of "community" have been neglected, apart from the spatial contexts. The conception of the term points out that a large portion of social relations, in addition to the importance of primary ties, is not organised in close-knit social networks. Even if the conception of personal networks does not necessarily run within the local presence of social relations, the transnational aspect of including different locations has only been partly covered so far. The dimension of transnationality, that is, the different national categories apart from the present country, have been disregarded.

Lubbers et al. (2007) manifest the relevance of both the composition and structure of personal networks to ethnic identification. Based on the ethnic-self identifications of migrants, they discuss the five network profiles that emerged out of the data. While there is one densely connected network linked to ethnic-exclusive identifications, the other heterogenous networks exhibit several different interpretations to the sense of belonging (ethnic-plural or transnational). Herz (2015) showcased that German migrants in Great Britain can be categorised into four personal communities depending on the transnationality of the ties, structural elements such as size and density, and emotional closeness. The basic hypothesis of these works is namely that there is a network effect and that both network composition and structure matter for how this effect is conceived. In this vein, the students' network patterns are formed by combining both structural and compositional information.

Students network in ways that are similar to many other individuals. In the book *Connecting in College: How Friendship Networks Matter for Academic and Social Success*, McCabe (2016) illustrates this by discussing how students form and maintain meaningful relationships in three different ways: close-packed group (tight-knitters), distributed groups (compartmentalisers), and meet someone new everyday (samplers). While she distinguishes between students' social and academic lives, I consider social lives as a single entity that encompasses various aspects in the support spectrum from instrumental help to social companionship. The network typologies are used as covariates to envision the support exchange, to check whether there is a network effect.

Students tend to have a preference for a specific medium or a specific mode of maintaining contact depending on the people in their networks who are contacted. They also share a few network characteristics according to which the networks are classified. To demonstrate both of these statements, cluster analysis[1] is used to illustrate types of network typologies based on the closeness measure, transnational measure, structural properties, and media profiles. The analysis shows four different types of personal network in the context of international students.

5.1 Four Network Typologies

I present typology, and discuss the different patterns of international students' personal networks in relation to media use in particular, as it is novel in the field. Previous studies have differentiated networks in terms of media use. There is a lack of discourse on the classification of personal communication media usage in students' networks. Walther and Boyd (2002) identified four clusters of online support while studying an online newsgroup. While this focused on the group features, some network studies have found network typologies based on individualistic media use (Boase 2008; Hogan 2009). Although the media features are the focus in the networks, somehow internet use was given more importance, and the clusters are segregated into heavy or light media use accordingly.

The aspect of transnationality of personal networks was considered previously on the basis of the demographic information of the students, or in connection with other relational characteristics. How can this aspect be combined with the media dimensions in the networks? The four patterns presented on the interpretive basis of descriptive features brings forth the connection between the media and transnationality aspects of personal networks. In the study, the international students are shown to be massive consumers of media in general. Besides considering media use among students, the network classification will include the frequency of that media use as well. It is assumed that the style of media use with an alter might depend on the structural embeddedness of the alter in the student's network.

Selection of Features

A handful of structural and compositional features of personal networks of international students are selected for the process of identifying different types of network. The aim of selection is to cover the structure with as few dimensions as possible, in order to gather as much theoretically and empirically interesting information on structure formations as possible (Wellman and Potter 1999). This theoretical consideration allows certain dimensions of the international student population—including their transnationality—to be relevant for the analysis. When viewed through the transnationality feature of the identified structure formations, the separate constellations are relatively different. Assumptions about the existence and structure of types of personal networks in the context of student mobility are not only theoretically derived in the following analysis, but also empirically defined. The patterns are centred on the differences in the structural properties.

A thrifty use and targeted selection of in-depth features is executed from an empirical perspective. However, type formations should not be overloaded[2] with a congregation of features used. All of the media factors (classic, neoteric, and established) variables were chosen along with the transnationality mean score (average proportion of transnational ties), closeness (degree of emotional intensity, that is, the average proportion of strong ties), size (number of relationships), and density (connectivity among the relationships) of the networks. To express the range of personal communities, the network size measure, which corresponds to the number of people in the networks, was chosen. This measure serves as the general description of the extent of personal networks (Campbell et al. 1986). To reflect the degree of connectedness of the networks, the density measure is used. However, the following difference should also provide opportunities for networks with regard to their media use. To represent both the use and frequency, media profiles are included, each countering to variables pertaining to media at the network level to see how networking styles are categorised through different media usage patterns. Transnationality was operationalised on the share of transnational relations. Emotional intensity played an important role in identifying the major people in a network. This measure is the scale of closeness, which measures from 0—*Not close* to 4—*Very close*.

The average network size of the students is seven, and individuals have an average density of 0.47 (Table 5.1). The proportion of transnational relations is about 37 per cent. The proportion of contact via face-to-face is the highest, being 95 per cent. The average contact using phone calls was 82 per cent, whereas letters and text were 21 per cent and 73 per cent, respectively. The measure of the standard deviation, that is, the variation of the contacts, was almost the same. The average contact using email and social networking sites were the same, at 69 per cent, and average IM contact was more or less the same, at 66 per cent. The average contact of each personal relationship using other platforms like Skype was 52 per cent. Since there are eight media dimensions used by the students to contact their network members at the relational level, media dimensions enter the different clusters in the form of media profiles. The three media profiles are classic (face-to-face interaction, phone calls, and text), neoteric (instant messaging and social networking), and established media (video chat and email).

Table 5.1 Descriptive values of cluster features

	M	SD	Min	Max
Classic media	0.07	0.6	−1.28	3.16
Neoteric media	0.04	0.66	−1.43	3.07
Established media	0.09	0.56	−1.31	3.52
Network size	7.05	4.54	1	27
Network density	0.47	0.29	0	1
Transnationality	0.37	0.31	0	1
Closeness	3.08	0.66	0	4

Like or Follow me

Like or Follow me networks have six members on average in each student's network, which is nearly the average of the network size of all of the international students. Type I is characterised by average level of connectedness in comparison to size (density = 0.35). This internal cohesion of the network which is less than the average network density is reflected in the highest average number of relationships. The characteristic of this pattern of network integration is at 60 per cent, having the highest proportion of relationships with people who do not live in the current country of residence (transnational). They exhibit high levels of emotional intensity as well, being the second highest among the different network types. Coming to the media factors, there is a heavy use of social networking sites and instant messaging. There is rarely exchange and use of classic media, which comprises face-to-face interactions, phone calls, and text. This is in accordance with the fact that they possess the highest number of transnational ties. This also accounts for the highest established media use—platforms such as Skype and email within the network type—and the second highest among the network types.

I will describe one network belonging to the respective type[3] for all of the typologies, to give an idea about the dimensions described for each international student,[4] along with a visualisation with respect to the features, media use variation, and support exchange. As seen in Fig. 5.1,[5] Aslan (who lives in South Africa) has only four people in his social network. A third of the people in his network know each other and it could be said that his network is moderately dense. His network consists of two non-transnational and two transnational ties: a supervisor and a colleague/friend living in South Africa, and two others (his parents) living in Turkey. While the local ties live in the same city, the Swiss supervisor (known for six years) and the Indian colleague (known for half a year) are considered to be close and somewhat close respectively. He probably met the supervisor during his university days, and the Indian colleague during the time since his arrival in South Africa.

Aslan from Turkey arrived in South Africa six months ago. In South Africa, he never socialises with other Turkish people who are his

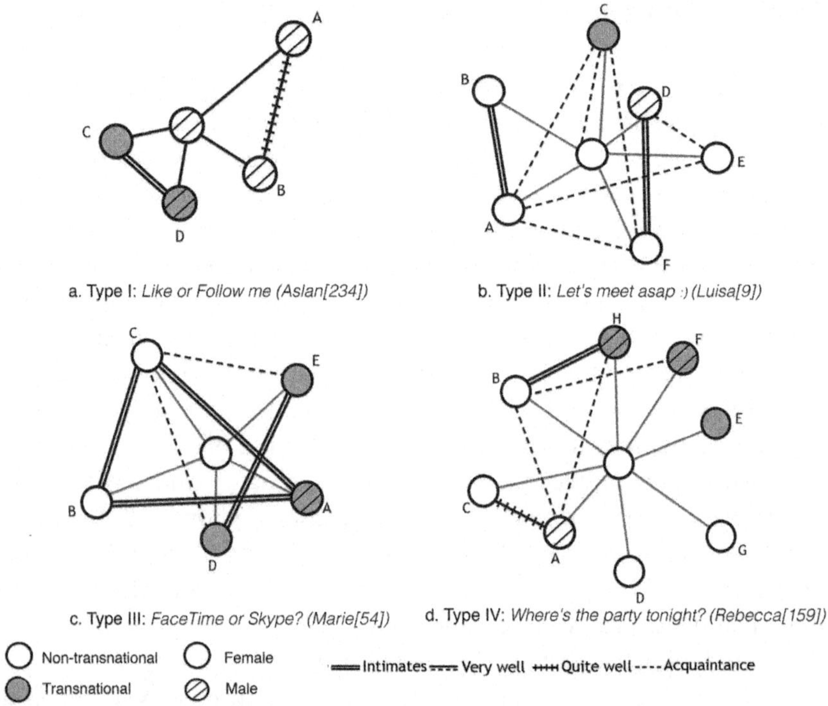

Fig. 5.1 Network typologies

co-nationals, but maintains contact with people in Turkey several times a week. Additionally, he socialises with people from various different countries on a daily basis, as he understands the local language very well. Despite being in a relationship, his spouse or partner is not reported in the network as one of the supportive ties. The media use strategies of Aslan are illustrated in the Fig. 5.2.[6] The figure shows the media patterns for each one of his network members, along with the closeness (between network members) indicator used in Fig. 5.1. The media channel visualisation is adapted from Hogan's study (2009) on networking patterns. The legend below the network figure explains the visualisation of different media tools and frequency. This legend diagram is applicable for the other diagrams demonstrating the media patterns of other networks.

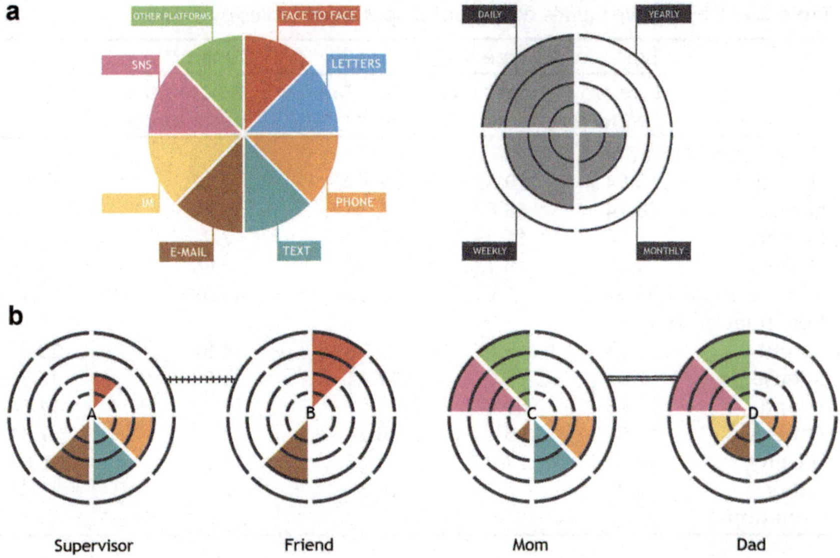

Fig. 5.2 **(A)** Networking patterns key **(B)** Media use in Aslan's network (*Like or Follow me*)

Although he has travelled around and been abroad before, he neither texts nor makes phone calls to contact people living outside South Africa. It is similar when it comes to people living in South Africa as well—except for phone calls which he makes fewer than five times a year—but he uses the internet for nine hours a day. With an equal proportion of transnational and non-transnational ties in Aslan's network, it is interesting to find that the media pattern is similar for the respective ties: face-to-face contact and emails are used for the local ties as they comprise his colleague and supervisor, whereas social networking sites and other platforms like Skype are used to maintain the relationship with his parents.

Let's meet asap :)

The second network type—which has the largest number of students (85)—has around six people in the network on average. As shown in Table 5.2, they exhibit the lowest proportion of transnational ties. They

Table 5.2 Descriptive values of temporal-spatial variables by cluster

	Type I *Like or Follow me*	Type II *Let's meet asap :)*	Type III *FaceTime or Skype?*	Type IV *Where's the party tonight?*	F
Geographical location					
Household	5.84	19.82	22.47	9.47	10.87
Local	28.64	48.82	26.34	35.61	13.38
Regional	1.96	11.33	2.52	7.2	5.94
National	4.03	8.12	4.08	2.65	2.48
Transnational	59.54	11.91	44.59	45.08	86.1
Role relationships					
Parent	15.07	5.57	26.79	4.94	23.7
Spouse	7.41	8.07	17.11	1.87	12.78
Friend	52.28	60.44	37.8	35.13	11.54
Other kin	12.5	6	16.2	4.6	7.51
Vicinity	14.64	27.06	8.16	11.72	8.03
Other relations	3.28	3.39	0.3	2	2.3

have exactly the average density, which indicates that half of the people in the networks know each other well. So it can be rightly said that this type is more local, consisting of people in the neighbourhood and the surroundings. This reflects quite well the proportion of relationships in the context of role relationships. This can be explained in another perspective: the transnational dimension of these personal communities in terms of the proportion of transnational relations is on average very low. They have close ties with a measure of 2.83, but not the strongest when compared to other network types. In terms of media use, classic media usage is the highest among the networks. This is totally understandable as the network is characterised by a very low number of transnational ties, and people get to see each other more often in this case. This does not act as a hindrance to usage of other media, and neoteric media are used on an average level. The established media use is the lowest among the networks, also explained by the fact that there is no need to Skype with someone when the ties are fairly local and nearby.

Luisa has been living in the Netherlands for four years now. She has been in contact with her friends and family back home in Germany every week since then. She is pursuing her master's and she is also single. There are six people in her network and nearly half of the people know each other, so the network is dense (0.47). She is a member of volunteer organisations consisting of both international students and Germans, her co-nationals, and also gets along with people there. She has been abroad before and socialises with other fellow Germans, as well as other international people every day.

To give an overview of Luisa's network, it primarily consists of her peers who are friends and people who live in the same apartment, that is, her flatmates, who constitute non-transnational or local ties. There are four Germans (two household ties and two local ties) in her network who live in the Netherlands. Unsurprisingly, face-to-face contact is mediated every day on a regular basis as they live in the same flat (Fig. 5.3). While she does not use a landline to call people living abroad, she uses phone calls and also texts them, both fewer than five times a year. Apart from this, there is no other regular communication through other media. She contacts people living in the Netherlands several times a month by mak-

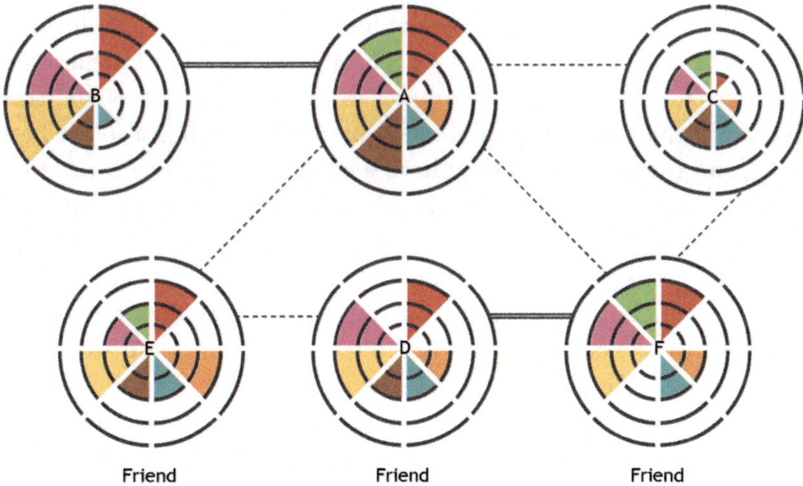

Fig. 5.3 Media use in Luisa's network (*Let's meet asap:)*)

ing calls and she texts them once a week. This monthly contact could arise in the case of emergency or even to provide information when Luisa is out of town. They do interact via email several times a week and, when it comes to social media, Luisa uses IM and social networking once a week.

Luisa communicates with one household tie through IM on a daily basis. Although there are two people living in the same flat, the forms of mediation of communication—apart from the inevitable face-to-face contact—differ largely between them. Despite the homogeneity in terms of origin and sharing the space, the closeness factor plays a vital role, that is, the closer the tie is to Luisa the more media are used for communication. There is just one transnational tie in the network, who is living in the US, and the ways of mediation are much fewer, as they meet face-to-face and make phone calls less than five times a year.

FaceTime or Skype?

Personal networks belonging to the Type III category are characterised by the lowest number of alters in their networks. They have four alters on average, and they have the highest density in that almost all the people in the network know each other quite well. Furthermore, the international students belonging to this category have the strongest ties in their networks (a measure of 3.59), which is also the highest among the networks. They have a slightly above-average number of transnational ties. This explains the behaviour of using other platforms such as Skype to stay connected with the members of their networks. Established media are used extensively in this network, and its usage is relatively high compared to other types of networks. Besides this, classic media use is the second highest, and there is an average use of neoteric media.

Marie has five people in her network: two local and three transnational ties. While two of the transnational ties belong to her home country (Philippines), one is in the Netherlands, the neighbouring country to

Belgium, where she currently resides. The neighbouring country tie is her boyfriend whom she meets once a month and maintains contact with mainly through neoteric media. The family ties—which consist of sibling and parent—live in their home country and are considered to be very close. There is a chance that this closeness factor arises due to cultural differences, as there is very little mediation for these ties.

Apart from letters, all of the other media channels are used to contact the boyfriend as well as the other two friends in the network (as shown in Fig. 5.4). While Marie meets one friend every day, she meets her other friend on a weekly basis. The boyfriend is the most frequently contacted person in the sense that all the media are used more frequently with him, compared to other members in the network. Communication through mobile phone (making phone calls and texting) is common to use with all the network members. Neoteric media (social networking sites and

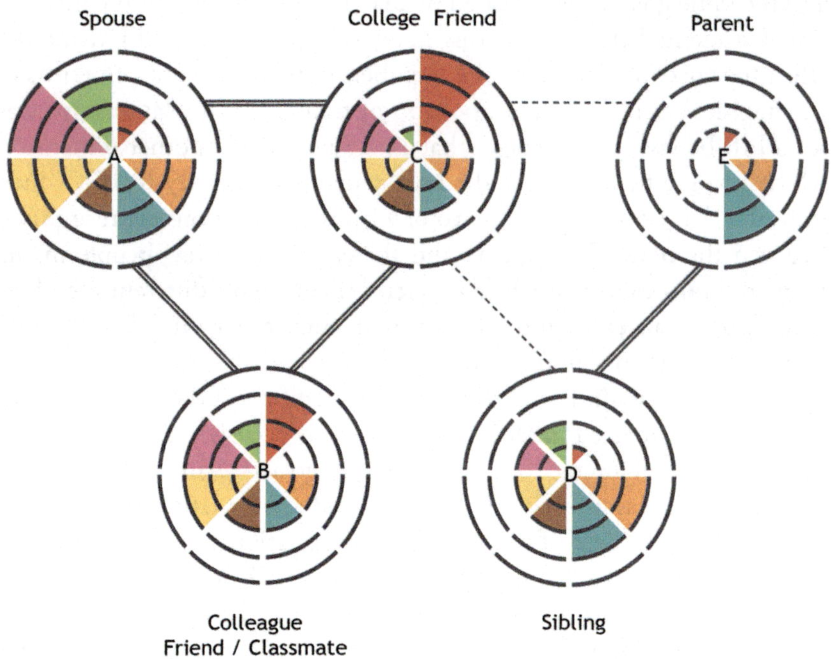

Fig. 5.4 Media use in Marie's network (*FaceTime or Skype?*)

IM) and established media (email and social platforms like Skype) are mostly used to connect on a monthly basis with everyone except the mother.

Where's the party tonight?

Personal networks of the fourth type differ clearly from the rest in two characteristics: large network size (15 people) and low media use. Another dimension—which is crucial and totally different from the others—is that it has the lowest density (0.16). So the *Where's the party tonight?* networks are very loosely knit (only two out of 20 persons in the networks know each other). With an average of 45 per cent, they have the second highest proportion of transnational relations. Coming to media use, classic media and neoteric media are the lowest among the networks: the students do not really use much social networking and instant messaging, and the same goes for established media. This illustrates that the international students belonging to this network type do not really make the effort to stay connected with the members of their networks. In terms of geographical distance, the proportion of transnational relationships was found to be less than average, that is, 45 per cent. Another dimension which is quite perceptible is the low value of the density (0.16), which indicates that on average only two of 11 possible relations are recognised between the network members and therefore only a few people in the network know each other. In the heterogeneous type, different members of networks can come into contact with each other due to the strong variation of relations in different contexts.

The low density indicates here that the members of these networks are mostly not connected independently of the ego. This may also apply to the transnational interactions, in which the ego acts as an intermediary or a broker and has the ability to bring different relationship contexts together. With a share of 37 per cent of transnational relations, on average two to three per network of relationships are connected to people who do not live in the same country of residence. This proportion of ties is the highest within the networks. While local ties are the second highest, national ties seem to be the lowest.

It is five years since Rebecca arrived in Finland. She is an active member of multiple organisations which consists of Germans, Finns, and various other international people. While pursuing a master's in Finland, she has contact with people in Germany several times a week. She socialises with German people several times a week but with people from other countries only once a week. She has never been abroad before. As she does not possess a landline, she uses a mobile phone to call and text her spouse and two other local friends on a weekly basis, whereas she contacts those living abroad less than five times a year.

She mentions 14 people in the survey but only eight people were selected for the name interpreters section. Out of eight people, only four live abroad and the other four live in the same country. So, it could be said that half of the ties are transnational and half are non-transnational. Although there are lots of people in the network, the network is not very dense in the sense that they hardly know each other (Fig. 5.1).

Apart from transnational ties, local ties comprise people living in the same household or city—not across the city or in another state. She speaks and understands Finnish quite well. Half of the networks comprise people of the same origin, that is, German. With a lot of people in the network, it can be assumed that the connections are mediated well using different modes of communication (see Fig. 5.5). On the contrary, except for her spouse, she uses media a negligible amount, that is, a lot of media are used but to a very small degree in terms of frequency.

5.2 Relation to Other Characteristics

While interesting aspects have been captured in the students' networks through essential features such as transnationality and media use, the presentation of the different patterns of personal communities could go one step further by relating the identified network formations to individual and relational characteristics. The transnationality is expressed not only in the consideration of transnational relationship constellations, but by the extent of the ties in terms of geographical distribution and a few features of mobility. The international students involved in transnational networks of relationships have different pat-

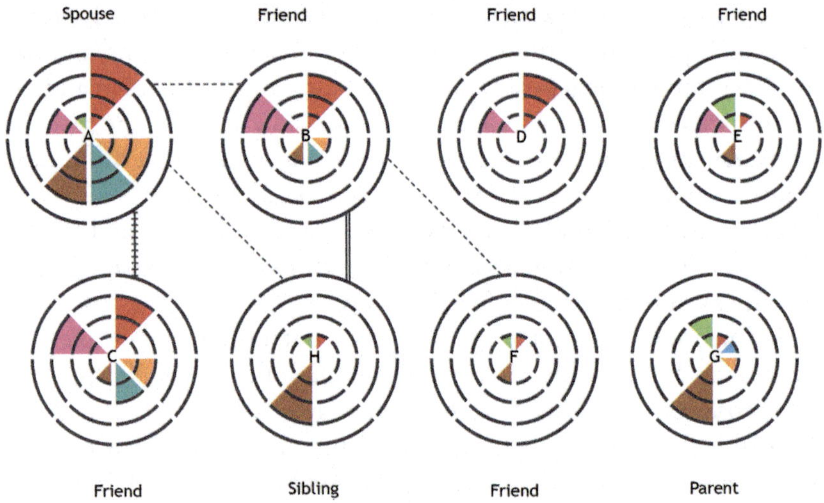

Fig. 5.5 Media use in Rebecca's network (*Where's the party tonight?*)

terns of activity in terms of cross-border practices. The patterns can be differentiated and explained more by a high degree of cross-border mobility, specific relationship to the origin, duration of a relationship and context of arrival. So, the four types of personal network identified—(I) *Like or Follow me*, (II) *Let's meet asap :)*, (III) *FaceTime or Skype?* and (IV) *Where's the party tonight?*—are correlated with the personal characteristics of the students. The following section therefore intends to monitor the comparability between the heterogeneous forms of the networks and their individual features. Subsequently, the four types of personal network are examined on the question of whether the formation is a condition for the provision of social support.

Geographical Distribution

Following the proportion of transnational ties among the networks, six per cent of the relatively average proportions of people live in the same household in the first network type (*Like or Follow me*). Over one quarter of the relationships are with people in the same neighbourhood or other neighbourhoods, but in the same city, both of which comprise local ties (28.6 per cent). It is clear that the transnational ties outnumber the ties living in the same country (regional and national ties comprise around five per cent). This demonstrates that even though the ties can be broadly classified according to their geographical location as transnational and non-transnational ties, the non-transnational ties encompass mostly local ties, which gives a new dimension to the non-transnational ties in general. It is also noteworthy that the *Like or Follow me?* networks consist of the lowest number of household ties compared to the other network types. As predicted while describing the *Let's meet asap :)* cluster based on the network features, there is the highest percentage of local ties in the networks (about 70 per cent of these relationships consist of people within the same household or in the same place/city). In this respect, contacts are mainly maintained at a small geographic-spatial distance. Among the students' networks, except for the household ties, they comprise the highest ratio of non-transnational ties (including local, regional, and national). Within this network type, most of the ties are in the same country.

As there are fewer people in the students' networks belonging to the *Like or Follow me* network, they are expected to be spatially concentrated, but reality proves otherwise, indicating that they do have far-flung ties. Despite this, they also succeed in having the largest proportion among the networks of ties in the same household. Although they have the highest household ties, they have the lowest local ties among the networks. They also belong to the second lowest category of regional as well as transnational ties. Apart from the household ties, they have the second highest national ties, something rarely seen in any of the other networks. As they have more tightly knit networks, they are presumed to have more partner-oriented networks living in the same household. In contrast, same-country ties outnumber transnational ties.

With the lowest density in the *Where's the party tonight?* network, people hardly know each other in the network and this is reflected by the closeness score (2.70) being the lowest among the students' networks. Out of all the clusters they have the highest number of people in the network that are spread all over. The students in this network are mostly looking for ephemeral relationships, so the network is aptly named

Where's the party tonight? Coming to the spatial extension and transnationality dimension, the proportion of people living in the same city (including the household ties) seems to be relatively high (45 per cent) compared to the proportion of transnational ties. Apart from the national and regional ties, transnational and local ties are equally distributed in the *Where's the party tonight?* networks.

Mobility

In general, all of the people in the students' networks have been in the current country of residence for more than one year, as explained in the descriptive section. The duration in the current country of residence plays an important role in meeting people and building relationships. Students belonging to the first network (*Like or Follow me*) arrived in the country of residence nearly two years ago (approximately 1.75 years). That is actually the lowest among the four network types. While the time of arrival plays an important role in determining new relationships, it could also be that the students already know people there. It could also be that friendships with old friends or acquaintances are reinforced. Nearly half of the people belonging to this network have lived abroad before. Students belonging to the *Let's meet asap :)* network have stayed the longest, with a duration of 2.8 years. There were some outliers with 11–14 years. The students belonging to the *FaceTime or Skype?* network have lived in the current country of residence for a comparatively long time, with the second highest duration of 2.64 years. Nearly half of the students in this network type have lived abroad before, as with Clusters I and II. The *Where's the party tonight?* network belong to the second lowest category when it comes to duration (time since arrival is around 1.77 years). There is no big difference between Clusters I and IV in terms of duration. At the same time, small variances within the type show that the networks represent a very consistent pattern. Most of the students belonging to this network have lived abroad, making it the highest of all (70 per cent).

Normative Context

Considering the role of relationships in *Like or Follow me* networks, parents, friends, other kin, vicinity ties, and other relations make up the second highest among the students' networks. At the same time, spouse relationships are the second lowest, and other relations do not make a major contribution, being the least when compared to relationships within the Type I cluster. Friends make up half of the networks within the cluster which is the largest proportion. The next largest proportions in *Like or Follow me* networks are primarily comprised of parent and vicinity ties. In *Let's meet asap :)* networks, friends play a crucial role and make up the largest proportion in the network among the clusters. Coming to the proximity role relationships, they are the highest as well. So the students belonging to this network do not have many familial ties, with other relations such as professor or ex-partner making up the highest among the clusters.

FaceTime or Skype? networks have the highest proportion of spouses. Along with the partners, other family members such as parents lead the proportion of ties among the clusters, making it a more family-oriented network. Friends are the second lowest (37 per cent) and the vicinity ties (nine per cent) are the lowest. Within the cluster, it is evident that it is basically family-oriented, and family relations altogether outnumber friends. As there are fewer people in the networks, it could be that the focus is mainly on the family. When the relationship context was observed in the *Where's the party tonight?* network, it was found that somehow the relationships were less distributed among themselves. Both relationships with parents and relationships with partners were the lowest among the clusters (five and two per cent). It was less family-oriented and more friend-oriented, as family and spouse category ties were the least among the other networks. At first glance, it is discernable that the ties are well distributed in the role relationships, but all belong to the lowest category among the clusters (spouse, parents and friends, and other kin being the lowest, and vicinity ties and other relations being the second lowest). There are not many familial ties within the cluster and friends and proximity relationships play quite an important role.

Internet Use

The *Like or Follow me* network exhibits the highest use of the internet, at nearly seven hours. One hypothesis could be that the more transnational the network, the more the need to be online to connect with the transnational ties. The time spent online by the students in *Let's meet asap :)* networks is about 5.80 hours a day, the second lowest among the clusters. Ties were made offline mostly and were lowest on connecting online. *FaceTime or Skype?* students use the internet for the second longest time. Spending nearly seven hours a day, they also meet people online, making this the second highest among the clusters.

Personal Characteristics

Students belonging to the *Like or Follow me* cluster are studying bachelor's and master's extensively, the second highest number among the clusters. PhD students were the lowest, equal to the Type II network, and the exchange students were also the lowest. Master's students are higher than 40 per cent within the cluster, and this reflects the descriptives as well. Coming to the relationship status among the international students of the *Like or Follow me* cluster, they have the lowest proportion of married people and also the second lowest number of people in a relationship. It could be said that they are equally distributed: 50 per cent are single and 50 per cent are either in a relationship or married. In terms of origin, there was a mix between Americans, Africans, Europeans, and Asians, and it could be said that this cluster consists of people belonging to all five regions.

The Type II *Let's meet asap :)* network has the highest number of students pursuing a bachelor's. While master's belong to the lowest category, similar to *Where's the party tonight* networks, PhDs also have the lowest proportion. As bachelor's degrees are being pursued by many in the cluster, it could be expected that there are a lot of exchange students as well who portray very similar characteristics to the bachelor's students. It was noted that exchange students belong to the second highest category among the networks. Most of the students in the *Let's meet asap :)* networks are in a relationship, making it the second highest, and single students make up the second lowest category among the clusters. It was seen that students in a relationship made up a huge portion within the network as well. In terms of the country of residence, there are a good amount of people living in America and Europe. It was also striking to see that there is a concentration of students studying in neighbouring countries (in the same continent); that is, there is not always a trans-Atlantic or trans-Pacific border crossing, and there are movements between countries such as Kenya and South Africa.

There is a high number of master's students in the *FaceTime or Skype?* network and the second highest number of PhD students, with a very small number of exchange students. This could be reflected in the duration of stay in the country of residence. As noticed during the discussion of spatial extension of the ties in the Type III network, *FaceTime or Skype?*, students in a relationship or married exceed the number of single students and there are many household ties. There are lot of Asians in the cluster, mainly from the Southeast Asian countries and the Indian subcontinent. It could be a culturally related factor that they are more family-oriented and also well-connected when taking an ethnocentric perspective. Most of the students are living in countries in Europe and Africa (Table 5.3).

In the fourth and final network *Where's the party tonight?* it is noteworthy that the students are single, and this ranks the highest among, as well as within, the cluster. Moreover, the lowest number of students in a relationship belong to this category. It could be said that they are mostly single and ready to mingle. This could possibly be one of the reasons that there are no extra efforts taken to maintain contact, and contacts are superficial in the network. The lowest duration in the current country of residence exhibited by this network gives an idea that the students are enrolled in study programmes which are not mainstream, in the sense of lower numbers of years. On the contrary, it is found that there is the highest number of PhD students in this cluster. Although there are very low numbers of bachelor's students, it was noticed that the network type has the highest number of exchange students. Looking at

Table 5.3 Descriptive values of social demographic variables by cluster

	Type I *Like or Follow me*	Type II *Let's meet asap :)*	Type III *FaceTime or Skype?*	Type IV *Where's the party tonight?*	F
Mean age	25.44	25.87	25.5	26.15	0.22
% Female	70	65	65	73	0.34
Duration in years	1.75	2.8	2.64	1.77	2.82
% Lived abroad before	48	46	50	70	1.95
Hours spent on internet	7.05	5.8	6.83	5.79	1.7
% Met online	12	7	10	9	1.04
Educational level					
% Bachelors	30	33	25	21	0.71
% Masters	40	36	42	36	0.18
% PhD	21	21	29	30	0.69
% Exchange	3	6	4	12	1.16
% Other	6	4	0	0	1.64
Relationship status					
% Single	51	42	34	61	2.24
% In a relationship	41	47	55	30	1.8
% Married	7	9	10	9	0.08
% Separated	0	1	0	0	0.58
Country of residence					
% Africa	23	22	23	3	2.37
% Americas	9	20	6	3	3.31
% Asia	3	5	2	0	0.97
% Europe	55	50	62	94	7.05
% Oceania	8	1	6	0	2.16
Country of birth					
% Africa	20	17	15	9	0.72
% Americas	10	12	6	21	1.48
% Asia	30	36	43	15	2.62
% Europe	36	34	35	51	1.11
% Oceania	3	0	0	3	1.35

the geographical as well as ethnic diversity, it is noticed that most of the students are Europeans and also live in Europe. This could be accounted for by programmes like Erasmus, and also because of easy visa regulations inside Europe.

Where's the party tonight? network is not heavily regulated by media use. They live for the moment, going to parties and meeting people. This is more likely when a person is so concentrated in their current living place. They have usual hangouts which are part of their routine life, with others who are also part of their everyday life. They do not really see any necessity in contacting and staying in touch with those who are not present in their surroundings or belong to their daily life at that point. Out of all the networks, the students who were the oldest (i.e. 26 years) belong to this cluster. It could be that people engage in a particular activity every week like aerobics, dancing, or language lessons. This opens a window of opportunity to meeting various people, but not necessarily to establishing relationships to the extent that phone numbers are exchanged. It could also be international associations that they are involved with and the timing could be fixed. Meeting lot of people is one thing and expecting to see them the next time is totally different.

5.3 Particularity Score

Not noted in the visualisation of the networks is that every network has its own strategy of contacting members and of communication between them. The four different networks demonstrate patterns of different dimensions, from media use to personal characteristics particular to the networks belonging to each cluster. Although the aspects of each network are perceptible through relating them to the personal characteristics of the individuals, certain features of the students are very individualistic, such that they cannot be categorised with other students. One such feature is the individual's style of using media according to the circumstances and the persons contacted in their respective networks.

Considering the *Like or Follow me* network, I notice that social networking site usage is popular, and the students have the highest number of transnational ties in their networks compared to the other three network typologies. I elaborate on this using the network of Zhang, who belongs to the Type I network. Zhang has lived in the US for six months and has four transnational and two non-transnational ties in his network. Social media such as social networking sites, IM, and other social platforms (mainly for video conference calls) are used on a daily basis to contact all of the transnational ties and one non-transnational tie. All of the transnational ties meet five times a year and phone calls are made every month, whereas the local ties are met every week and called every month. I ascertain that the media use in Zhang's network is not the same as that in Aslan's network, who also belongs to the Type I network. It is evident that each network has its own characteristics despite the partition into four networks.

The variation in media use can be determined using the particularity score as proposed by Hogan (2009). The differences in media usage across networks is calculated by identifying the distances between the alters (network members) and ego (international student in this case) for every single network and then this measure is compared across other networks. This quantitative measure, which was developed against a background of the logic of multidimensional scaling, is the average of the pairwise distances in a network.[7] Therefore, if there is a small distance between the ego and the alters, it is more likely that there is much less variation in the media use. In other words, the interaction between the network and student is in a similar fashion. On the other hand, if there is a huge variation and there are different trends within the network using the same media with different frequencies, or different media, then the distance is high.

While the overall patterns of media use in the students' networks were deducted using cluster analysis, the particularity score envisions the differences within the networks. Regression was carried out to find the factors affecting the particularity score, that is, variation in the media use and frequency. Although individual characteristics such as age, gender, education, duration, and internet use were considered, all of the structural properties seem to be influencing the score.

Particularity is the variation of the media usage pattern. The higher the particularity score, the higher the variation in the media use within the network between the alters. The size and degree have a positive significant effect, conveying that the bigger the size of the networks, the higher the particularity score. So, if there are many people in the network, it is likely that the individual decides to have various media use patterns with different people. Network density seems to have a negative significant effect, in that the higher the density, the lower the particularity score, saying that if more people know each other, they use similar patterns in using different media with a set of people in a similar manner. A good exemplar could be a person having different subgroups pertaining to different contexts in their networks, where there is a similar pattern of using, for example, Skype with family members at a particular time according to the time zone, a WhatsApp group and irregular phone calls for school friends, and Facebook and texting for local college mates.

Notes

1. A *k*-mean cluster analysis was run on all 291 students ($N = 231$, the remaining 60 had missing values).
2. The individual network characteristics correlate more or less with each other and might lead to erroneous conclusions when this is not observed. The exclusion of variables which are not dependent on each other statistically prevents the dimension shown by the correlated variables, which are over-represented in the analysis. For example, as there is a significant relationship between the proportion of transnational relationships and the proportion of relationships with home country ties ($r = 0.66$, $p < 0.001$), home country ties were not included, and nor was the relationship with familial ties. Overall, no variables have been included which have a correlation with other features of more than $r = 0.65$.
3. Networks were chosen according to the number of the cluster that the particular network was assigned and the deviation from the cluster centre in SPSS. The one that deviated least from the centre which is most typical of that particular cluster was selected for visualisation.
4. All the names of the respondents (Aslan [Like or Follow me?], Luisa [Let's meet asap :)], Marie [FaceTime or Skype?], Rebecca [Where's the party tonight?]) for whom the networks are visualised are anonymised.
5. The number next to the name of the respondent indicates the case number in the data.
6. The colours corresponding to the different media channels in the legend are as follows: red—face-to-face, blue—letters, orange—phone calls, teal green—text/SMS, brown—email, yellow—IM, pink—SNS, lemon green—other platforms.
7. Distance mentioned here is Euclidean distance and is calculated as the root of the sum of the squares of the variables. For n cases, there are $(n\ (n - 1)) = 2$ comparisons.

References

Boase, J. (2008). Personal networks and the personal communication system: Using multiple media to connect. *Information, Communication & Society, 11*(4), 490–508.

Campbell, K. E., Marsden, P. V., & Hurlbert, J. S. (1986). Social resources and socioeconomic status. *Social Networks, 8*(1), 97–117.

Freeman, L. (2004). *The development of social network analysis: A study in the sociology of science*. Vancouver, CA: Empirical Press.

Herz, A. (2015). Relational constitution of social support in migrants' transnational personal communities. *Social Networks, 40*, 64–74.

Hogan, B. J. (2009). *Networking in everyday life*. Toronto, ON, Canada: University of Toronto.

Lubbers, M. J., Molina, J. L., & McCarty, C. (2007). Personal networks and ethnic identifications the case of migrants in Spain. *International Sociology, 22*(6), 721–741.

McCabe, J. M. (2016). *Connecting in college: How friendship networks matter for academic and social success*. University of Chicago Press.

Walther, J. B., & Boyd, S. (2002). Attraction to computer-mediated social support. In C. A. Lin & D. Atkin (Eds.), *Communication technology and society: Audience adoption and uses* (pp. 153–188). Cresskill, NJ: Hampton.

Wellman, B. (1979). The community question: The intimate networks of East Yorkers. *American Journal of Sociology, 84*(5), 1201–1231.

Wellman, B. (1988). The community question re-evaluated. In M. P. Smith (Ed.), *Power, community and the city* (pp. 81–107). New Brunswick, NJ: Transaction Books.

Wellman, B., & Potter, S. (1999). The elements of personal communities. In B. Wellman (Ed.), *Networks in the global village* (pp. 49–82). Boulder, CO: Westview Press.

6

Determinants of Social Support

In the previous chapter, I identified different types of personal networks of international students spread across many countries. The characteristics of the students' personal networks such as structure, transnationality, and media use defined the different types of network. Following this, I focused on the question of how provision of social support takes place. The social lives of the international students are given closer consideration through a certain function of the networks, that is, social support exchanged. Does this support exchange vary according to the network types? I will examine this by looking at the network typologies in relation to support exchange among the international students.

6.1 Process of Social Support Exchange

Let us first consider an example for each network type, for the purpose of illustrating the support flow. Aslan belongs to the *Like or Follow me* network, which is characterised by average network size and density in the study and substantial use of social media. As Fig. 6.1a shows, Aslan receives emotional support from all of the relationships in his network (his parents, colleague, and supervisor), but he reciprocates emotional

R. Kanagavel, *The Social Lives of Networked Students*,
https://doi.org/10.1007/978-3-319-96199-6_6

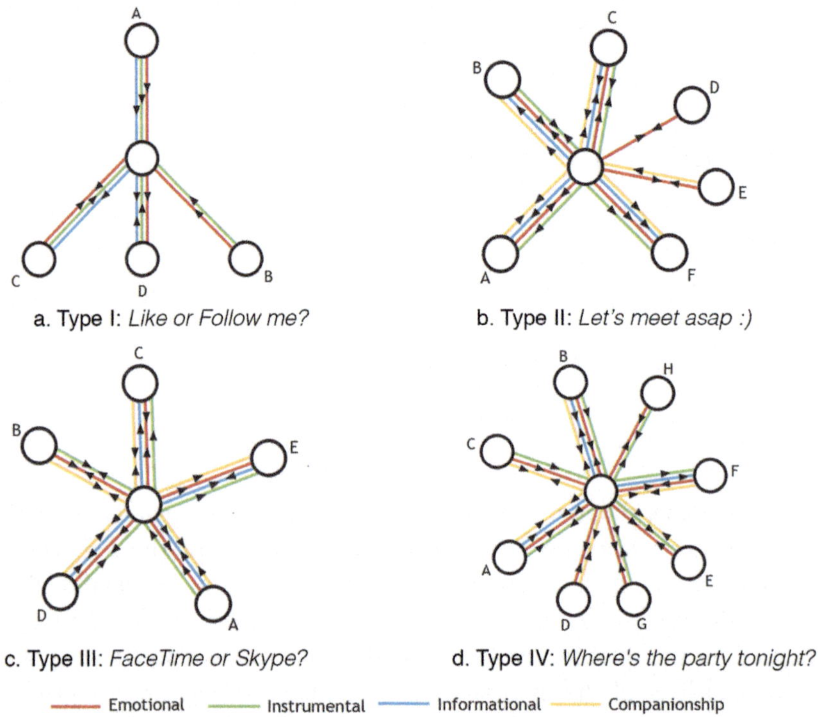

Fig. 6.1 Support exchange in networks a. Type I: *Like or Follow me?* b. Type II: *Let's meet asap :)* c. Type III: *FaceTime or Skype?* d. Type IV: *Where's the party tonight?*

support to only half of the people (i.e. two alters) in the network. Instrumental support, which comprises financial aid or practical help such as moving furniture or picking up something at the store (Offer and Fischer 2018), is received from all members of the network irrespective of their geographical location, but none is provided back by him. This is justifiable as his network is constituted of both transnational and local ties who can provide financial support and practical help respectively. Both emotional and instrumental support are acquired from all ties in his network. It is therefore observed that Aslan is at the receiving end of this support, except for one occasion where he provided informational support to one person in his network. It is noteworthy that there is no exchange of social companionship.

Luisa, who belongs to *Let's meet asap :)* network category, does not get a large amount of support. Students belonging to this network typology are confined to their local settings. They are less transnational in the sense that they do not have many ties with those who live abroad. They have more local ties, and meeting people in the local neighbourhood has become a routine for those in this category. Apart from one friend hanging out and sharing leisure time with Luisa, no other members in her network necessarily act as support resources unless it is reciprocated from Luisa herself. Out of all the ties, the transnational tie is the only one that provides multistranded support. This tie shares three types of directed connections of support (instrumental, informational, and leisure) with Luisa. In Luisa's network it is observed that she is the one who actively provides all kinds of support to two thirds of her ties (four out of six). The amount of emotional support provided by Luisa to others outnumbers the emotional support she receives.

The third type of cluster, which is illustrated through Marie's network (see Fig. 6.1c), is less likely to get emotional support. They are tightly bound in terms of emotional intensity, so they already enjoy their space in a relaxed situation. They are so close that they hardly recognise any problem or issue within the close-knit compassionate world within which they reside. They are dwelling in a comfortable situation in which emotional support is not recognised as support anymore. The prominent point about support exchange in this network is that almost all other kinds of support are received by Marie and returned to the members, except for social companionship and instrumental support for each tie respectively.

The last type of network *Where's the party tonight?* is characterised by a high number of network members and low media use. Rebecca, whose network belongs to this category, receives instrumental support from five of her network members (see Fig. 6.1d). Informational support exchange is fairly low. Although weak ties provide informational support, changes in situation and people at different times mean they are probably less likely to give and receive informational support. Six out of eight ties have mutual exchange of emotional support and social companionship with Rebecca.

6.2 Prediction of Social Support at the Network Level

The different forms of social support resources built as students' personal networks vary in each network typology, along with the degree of transnationality and media use. The social support research reflects on the assumptions of structural analysis (Wellman 1988b), according to which dyadic relationships, through their embeddedness in social structures, are used as explanatory principles. Although I showcased support flow through students belonging to each network category, I probe how the different structures of each type of personal network predicted differences in social support. The structuring of the international students' networks serves as infrastructures for providing resources and is measured by a level of social support. Using single-factor analysis of variance method, I check whether the four network typologies differ in the average proportions of supportive relationships (emotional, instrumental, informational, and social companionship).

Figure 6.2 shows that the support type that is most frequently provided is emotional support, with an average of 47.6 per cent. The reception of emotional support varies from 40 to 60 per cent across different types of network, with the *Like or Follow me* network having the highest percentage. Instrumental support is received by the students from about a third of relationships on average. The spatially-concentrated *Let's meet asap :)* networks are involved in a higher level of instrumental support, much like the concentrated and far-flung *Like or Follow me* network. They are on par with each other at 34 per cent. This contrasts with the socialising *Where's the party tonight?* networks, which focus on meeting new people rather than maintaining lots of contacts, and exhibit low media use. Informational support is reported for an average of about 30 per cent, and *Like or Follow me* networks seem to have the highest proportion. There is not much difference in receiving informational support in all the four networks. Leisure time is spent with 56 per cent of the reported relationships. With nearly 50 per cent of social companionship received, *Where's the party tonight?* network, which is the type that has many people in an average network, seems to be the highest in comparison to the other networks.

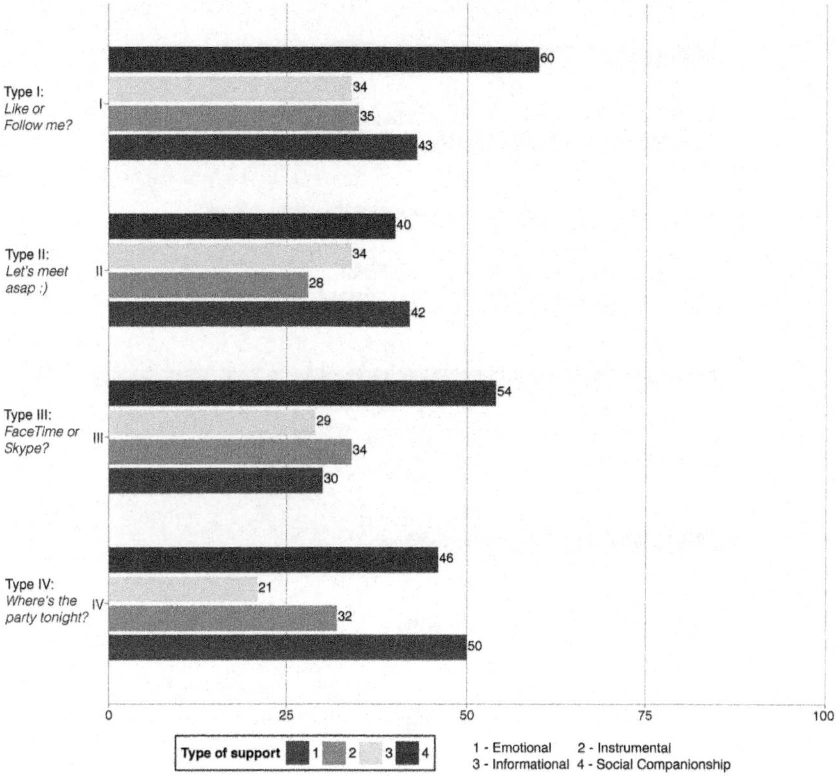

Fig. 6.2 Clusters (Type I—*Like or Follow me?*, Type II—*Let's meet asap :)*, Type III—*FaceTime or Skype?*, Type IV—*Where's the party tonight?*) by the support dimensions received (1-Emotional support, 2-Instrumental support, 3-Instrumental support, 4-Social companionship)

Differences are manifested clearly in terms of the instrumental and emotional dimensions, especially between Type I (*Like or Follow me*) and Type IV (*Where's the party tonight?*) networks. Type II (*Let's meet asap :)*) and Type III (*FaceTime or Skype?*) networks are somewhat parallel to each other when it comes to informational and instrumental support.

Let us now look at the support given, as we did with the dimensions of support received. As seen in Fig. 6.3, the proportion of relationships that are given emotional support by the students exceeds 88 per cent at its highest point, which is exhibited by the Type III *FaceTime or Skype?* net-

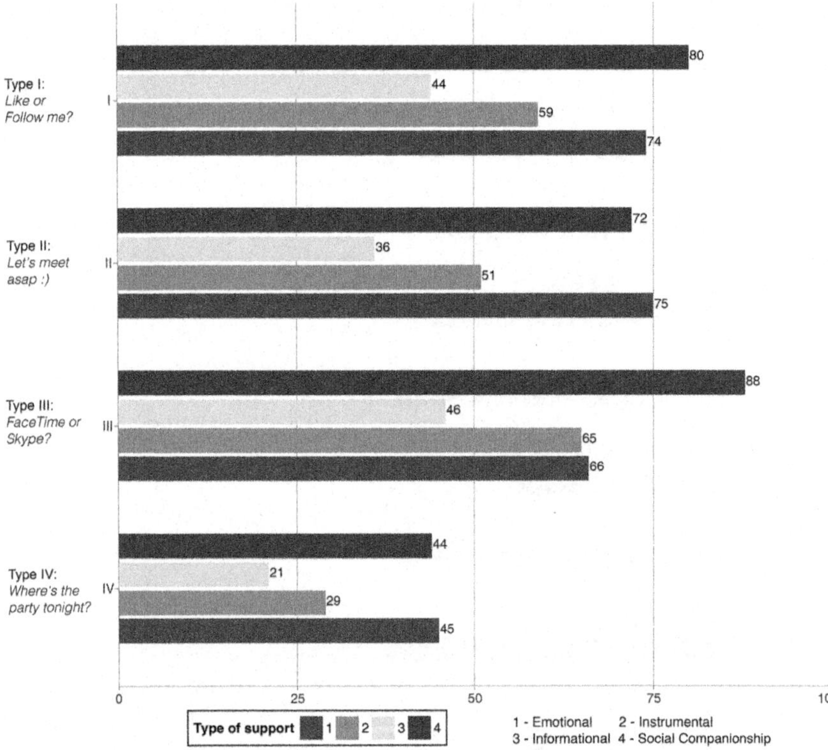

Fig. 6.3 Clusters (Type I—*Like or Follow me?*, Type II—*Let's meet asap :)*, Type III—*FaceTime or Skype?*, Type IV—*Where's the party tonight?*) by the support dimensions given (1-Emotional support, 2-Instrumental support, 3-Instrumental support, 4-Social companionship)

works. Instrumental support is given by international students to 36 per cent of the members of their network on average, with *FaceTime or Skype* networks being the highest (around 65 per cent). Along the same lines, informational assistance is given to an average of 51 per cent of the relationships, and the Type II cluster seems to have the highest proportion. Students belonging to the spatially-concentrated *Let's meet asap :)* networks spent leisure time or pursued a hobby with nearly 75 per cent of the relationships. This makes sense as students in this network meet the members of their network more often.

In terms of support given by the students to their network members, it was found that more pairs of networks were different ($p < 0.05$) when tested for significance. All network pairs, except *Like or Follow me* network, when related with *Let's Meet asap :)* network and *FaceTime or Skype?* network, were different in terms of emotional support. The fourth type of network, *Where's the party tonight?* differed significantly from all the other network types in instrumental as well as informational support given. Regarding social companionship, all network pairs, except the *Like or Follow me* and *Let's Meet asap :)* networks, showed significant differences.

Comparison of the means show that different types of networks differ in the proportion of supportive relationships received as well as given. Extending this exploration of support exchange at the network level to the various aspects of relationships, I investigate the interesting phenomenon of support multiplexity at the relational level.

6.3 Exploring Support Multiplexity

Multiplexity is the intersection of different roles or exchanges taking place within a relationship. The relational distribution of personal networks shows that active personal networks are composed of a variety of ties. As conventional studies on social networks developed during the 1950s, sociologists became interested in the concept of network multiplexity (Mitchell 1969). For example, a multiplex relationship could be between flatmates who are also colleagues, or between relatives who also go to the gym together.

Support multiplexity takes place when more than one support dimension is exchanged in a relationship between two individuals, in this study between international students and their network members. Different types of content pertaining to support, such as social companionship or emotional support, are overlapped within the same tie, leading to exchange of support multiplexity. Although multiplexity and exchange have long been studied as features of networks, they have not been examined meticulously (Skvoretz and Agneessens 2007).

The context of a relationship indicates the extent to which that relationship can be combined with different features. Relationships have a propensity to exist in a separate sphere of social life, where the student is affiliated to one specific bevy of connections, and each bevy is related to one distinct social sphere: colleagues, community members, or even family. The traditional method of having a multiplex relationship could be with people who live in the same vicinity or grew up together in the same surroundings. Originally, Gluckman (1955) introduced the term to denote the co-existence of different normative elements in a social relationship. He pointed out the co-occurrence of distinct social roles in a dyad, or role-based multiplexity. For example, a father and son who are also employer and employee.

Dyadic relationships can be exhibited in the case of friendships that are affiliated in three major roles: kin, neighbour, and co-worker (Verbrugge 1979). Various reasons such as limited opportunities and segregation of networks persisted for a long time, but today this scenario is fading away with the proliferation of activities and people in one's network, which tend to be more dynamic and flexible. This is proven in the study as only approximately three per cent of the international students had multiplex relationships, that is, associated with more than one relational context.

Kapferer (1969) offers a second definition of tie multiplexity: the overlap of different exchanges and activities in a social relationship. Thus, a multistranded or multiplex relationship serves multiple purposes and contains more than "one focus of interaction or content area" (Fischer 1982). This is exchange multiplexity. Several other dimensions can be discussed, but not on the level of personal relationships. In that case, multiplex ties exist when two people have two or more memberships in common, for instance, and more on the level of organisations.

The number of social contexts that individuals tend to share (i.e. role multiplexity) might influence the number of support dimensions that they exchange, which accounts for support multiplexity. Networks with multiplex ties are more likely to result in the mobilisation of support, especially in times of need, because multiplex relationships by definition have multiple bases of interaction (Wellman and Wortley 1990).

The exchange of many support resources between two people might influence forming or breaking other relationships in a network. In network terms, closure might take place through triads, which will further kindle the ties to be transitive. For example, if student A shares personal problems (emotional support) and spends leisure time often (social companionship) with student B, while also engaging in social activities with student C frequently, student B and student C might also hang out together through A. This transitivity might enhance reciprocal multiplexity, which in turn can act as a source of reciprocal obligations, mutual expectations, and trustworthiness, as contended by Coleman (1988). So, student B or C tends to help or share personal problems or initiates spending leisure time with student A. Responsibilities or duties in the form of obligations may arise when the social spheres are shared and people belonging to different spheres tend to share tasks and help each other. This is more likely to arise between persons who have different types of relations at the same time. In general, more than a specific exchange of one favour for another, multiplexity facilitates relationships in which reciprocity takes place more easily. On that account, I examine the multiplexity of support dimensions both received and given.

Uniplex and Multiplex Relationships

Network relationships which contain only one support resource (exchange of emotional support) or role (friendship) are uniplex or single-stranded ties. Those that involve two or more contents (friendship and colleague) are multiplex links (Barnes 1972). If the relationship extends to other forms of support, not confined to emotional support, but beyond material support to spending leisure time, then this relationship is referred to as multiplex or multistranded.

Table 6.1 Uniplexity vs. multiplexity for relationships (support received $n = 1696$, support given $n = 1372$)

	Support received		Support given	
Number of dimensions	%	$n = 1696$	%	$n = 1372$
1	56	*Uniplex*: 56.0	17.9	
2	20.1	*Multiplex*: 44.0	24	
3	13.9		25.7	
4	10		32.4	

When I evaluated support, both given and received, at the network level the support given transcends the support received (see Table 6.1). In terms of support received by the international students from their networks, 56 per cent and 44 per cent of the relationships are uniplex and multiplex respectively. In the case of reciprocated support, that is, support given from the student, approximately 82 per cent and 18 per cent of the relationships were multiplex and uniplex respectively. Nearly half of the reported relationships overlap with different dimensions of social support.

The perception of the students, that they give more support than they receive, is in line with support research wherein the perception of reciprocal social exchanges is associated with higher life satisfaction (Antonucci et al. 1997). The degree to which this assessment of relationships as reciprocal is based on the time they have known their network members, active participation, frequency of contact, and interactions can only be speculated on.

Test for Multiplex Support

Coleman (1988) puts forth two prominent features of multiplex relationships: density and reciprocity. He claims that multiplex relationships, as compared to uniplex relationships, are a feature of dense and tightly knit networks. Density tends to correlate multiplexity as per the claim that everyone in the network knows each other and are more likely to meet when there is overlap in social spheres through which the student has been connected to their network members. If the student's flatmates are also schoolmates sharing the same classroom, then it is more likely that the people belonging to these two different spheres will meet and gain a higher level of intimacy, thus allowing the interaction between support multiplexity and density. This process takes place here as well, as it is noticed in the study that there is a negative correlation between the multiplexity in terms of role relationships, and density of the international students' networks. This corresponds to the fact that if the student's social spheres do not overlap, thus facilitating a meet-up between people in their networks, then the student will more likely be a broker between unconnected groups or subgroups which will be consonant to different spheres, causing structural holes. I hypothesise that highly dense networks provide and receive more social support.

Emotional intensity measured by the closeness factor is often included with other indicators of tie strength (Marsden and Campbell 1984) but is less focused when it comes to multiplexity (Wellman 1988a). Network research has proved that multiplexity is a key characteristic of strong ties, which directly facilitates the provision of more support. As closeness was relevant and crucial at the structural level, I presume strong relationships in a student's network facilitate multistranded support exchange.

The social sphere which is around the international student, that is, the vicinity role relationships (refer to Chap. 4) sharing the same vicinity or locality, are easily accessible (Marsden and Campbell 1984). Grossetti (2007) studied the influence of mobility on social support and concluded that it takes two years to form local ties. Chapter 4 showed that most of the ties in the family are transnational. Thus, it can be assumed that they provide specialised types of support such as emotional support, instrumental support, informational support, or social companionship individually, and that the people sharing the same social context as the international student, be it in school or neighbourhood, give and receive multistranded support.

Following the assumption that vicinity role relationships play a part in providing and receiving multistranded support, it is presumed that different dimensions of support can be experienced when co-present. This in turn proposes that the transnational support is uniplex and that transnational ties serve a unique purpose. Media use might vary the necessity of co-presence for multiplex support provision. When the media profiles used to connect with network members are interrelated with the proportion of transnational ties in a network, the dynamics associated with co-presence in a network come to light.

For the purpose of this study I presume that dynamics in media used for connecting with people will be different than networking at the individual level. Each media profile, which measures media use and frequency, consists of more than one medium. All three media profiles (classic, neoteric, and established media) gratify the needs of the student in different ways. They are alleged to amend the necessity of co-presence as they are combined with a few other media dimensions for support exchange.

Multilevel Model of Social Support

I test the theory of whether network characteristics such as density, tie strength, geographical location, and use of certain media profiles lead to increased provision of support dimensions from the network members to the international students and vice versa. Research has shown that students actively regulate their social accessibility by maintaining higher levels of access to those with whom they feel close (in terms of proximity as well as closeness intensity). However, there are practical reasons why students use certain media with their friends and family. They may be using the same media as the friend for example, which facilitates more frequent contact. I consider all measures one by one and together, and determine which ones make an important contribution to understanding how the support provision works.

Transmissions of social support are properties of both the relationships and the network structure, that is, connections among relationships of personal communities. The individual self-regulated arrangements, the dyads having interpersonal communication, and the opportunities postulated by networks with different sorts of structure and composition together can have an impact on support. I evaluate the provision of social support, be it unistranded or multistranded, from a perspective on personal communities which examines both the relational and structural characteristics using multilevel regression analysis[1] (see Multilevel Model of Support section in Appendix A Methodology). To explore the networks more closely, I devote the following section to exploring the network and the relational levels in conjunction. While looking at the dimensions at both levels, I analyse how relationships are mediated and contacted, how students cope with the distance, how integrated they become in their country of residence, and how support takes place through personal relationships in various forms, both received and given.

In the analysis of ego-centred network data, two levels of analysis are used: the relational level and the network level. The social relations (level 1) are the unit of analysis, which are thought to be embedded within personal networks (level 2). A relationship, whether specialised or multi-stranded (i.e. providing more than one type of support), is explained through its effects on different levels: relational or alter-level (level 1) and individual and network properties or ego-level (level 2), that is, the structural aspects of personal communities. As such, not only do individuals like to know which kinds of people (an individual-level analysis) and relationships (a tie-level analysis) are pertinent for providing different kinds of support, but also the extent to which their social networks as a whole can support them (a network-level analysis) (Wellman and Frank 2001).

I assess whether there is sufficient variance between networks in order to consider using a multilevel model. This is especially the case when considering media use, since it differs largely from student to student—for example, some students do not have a smartphone. This does not necessarily mean that media can substitute for one another: students who buy a laptop do not give up their landline phones. Many studies have reasonably shown that email and instant messaging seem to add on to other forms of communication rather than substituting for them (Carrasco and Miller 2006; Quan-Haase and Wellman 2006). As such, it is necessary to take into account this variation among networks. As expected, the variance indicates that the consideration of multilevel models is appropriate.

At the relational (alter) level, I choose properties such as media profiles, homophily, geographical location, normative roles, and tie strength, whereas at the network level I consider student demographic information, transnationality, network size, and density.

Although I discuss internet use and media dimensions in the form of clusters, it is always better to comprehend the interaction with the support in their raw factor form. The three media profiles—classic media, neoteric media, and established media—produced through factor analysis are considered. Homophily, the tendency to associate with people with similar characteristics, is an important aspect of social networks. Along with the basic demographics, I also include features that indicate whether the student and the network member, be it friend or classmate, were of the same sex and same age. As 43 per cent of the students' networks comprised friends on average, and university friends are likely to be of similar age, it is appropriate to choose three years as a level of magnitude for measuring homophily. Therefore alters, that is, people in the students' networks three years younger or older than the students themselves, are considered to be homophilous relations. Furthermore, the geographical and national categories are chosen to see the nature of homophily in the networks. Thus, same country of residence and country of origin are taken into account.

Transnational social network analysis allows analysis of people's activities spanning borders. To measure transnational relations, I categorised the relationships to know where the ties are currently residing in order to understand the spread of the network (refer Chap. 2). The alters' geographical location is considered in the model at the relational level. Transnational relationships are ties living abroad, national ties are ties living in another state of the same country, and regional ties are ties living in the same state. For example a friend of mine living in Hameln would be considered a regional tie as Hannover and Hameln are in the same state of Lower Saxony. Local ties comprise both ties living in the city and those in the nearest area or neighbourhood. Even though household ties can be categorised under local ties, they have a category to themselves.

As Granovetter (1977) notices, tie strength could encompass various dimensions of ties. Here I choose the duration of the relationship shared with the network member. As the duration of the relationship is dependent on each person in the network, it is considered to be a relational variable instead of a network variable in the models. The role relationship contents of the ties in the networks is also considered. I choose five normative contexts that make up a huge portion of the students' networks (Chap. 4): spouse/partner, family, friends, vicinity (comprising colleagues, neighbours, classmates, and flatmates), and other relationships.

Coming to the network level dimensions, student demographic information such as age and gender were added to the models. Considering the student population, it is an interesting take on how they share, receive, and provide support depending on their network members' characteristics such as age and gender. Additionally, time since arrival is another important aspect in a student's life in the new host country as this temporal dimension is a good measure for integration in the country of residence as well as the time required to build relationships that satisfy the needs of the respondents. The proportion of strong ties, which is an important dimension of tie strength, is examined at the network level. This involves the scale of closeness, and the average closeness of the ties predominantly falls into the category of either very close or close (see Chap. 2).

As there are fewer people in international students' personal networks, it is better to consider three important dimensions: density, alter degree, and size of the network. Size and density of the network refers to the number of alters, that is, people in the network and the interconnectedness between the alters in the network (see Chap. 2). Alter degree is the number of connections an alter has in the network. Besides closeness factor, the other compositional measure I look at is the proportion of transnational ties in a network.

Apart from this, I also examine cross-level interactions between media profiles and transnationality of the networks. This is an interesting aspect which can be utilised while constructing multilevel models. While the media factors were considered at the relational level, the transnational context of having the proportion of transnational ties in a network was at the network level. As the type and frequency of the media used and the proportion of transnational ties varies at two levels, it would be interesting to see whether they influence each other for the provision of support.

6.4 Discussion

The socio-demographic characteristics do not have an impact on the support received, and only age homophily seems to exert influence on support given: ties who are more or less the same age as the respondent are given more support. When it comes to the gender aspect in support, the question of asking for support or getting help comes up. My results indicate that women tend to give more support as compared to male students. But there is no significance at the end, proving that in this case it is difficult to distinguish between the qualities associated with support. Support structures differ in terms of gender, and students tend to communicate differently when it comes to support. Gender can have different perspectives/aspects and influence support differently.

Although homophily is considered to be an important aspect of the support flow in the network, it does not play a vital role in the networks of international students. This might be different when the support received or given is specialised or unistranded. It is expected that many people from the same country of origin feel the need to support each other. Alternatively, sharing information or personal matters among the same gender could have an influence but may not be multistranded in the same sense. That being said, age homophily tends to strike a chord with multistranded support given. The indifference of homophily (with the exception of age) for support given is accounted for by the fact that when someone is abroad, they mingle with people from different countries and are open to other cultures, and are curious to make inter-cultural connections rather than adhering to those of their own background.

Coming to the structural constituents in a network, the duration of a relationship could account for tie strength. The longer the relationship exists, the lower the probability of receiving multiple kinds of support. This could mainly relate to the new everyday life of an international student. The longer you know someone and get acquainted to a place, the less support is sought from other people. Any activity, for example borrowing a book from the library, going to a supermarket, visiting a doctor, or going shopping, needs help and support from the people living in the vicinity before it becomes routine. One assumption is that long relationships probably with family or friends from school, and there is less probability that family and long-term relations reside in the same country as the international student. This does not really mean that they provide no support: most likely the support which they provide is emotional support which is special and unistranded. But it is less likely that all support is offered from the same people under the same circumstances.

The number of local or transnational ties might strongly influence the duration of the relationship. When new to a country, there are no prolonged relationships at the beginning and the support is gained mostly from weak or ephemeral relationships. Somehow the tasks or the support sought during such times are divided and shared according to the person whom the respondent thinks can help. For example, at the beginning of university life, a flatmate might provide all the information necessary or help with tasks, but as time passes, and after getting to know more and new people, the support sought is spread or split such that the original person is no longer asked or referred to for help. With more time in the residing country, more relationships are formed, which in turn is the reason for support being reduced because of opportunities being spread across different people. This is synonymous with the reverse effect in the context of international student mobility. The longer a person stays, the more likely there are chances to meet new people and build relationships which last for a long time, which in turn increases the number of local ties. This means that there is no necessity to ask the same person for support or help.

The intensity of closeness can be inversely proportional to the duration of the relationship or even the time since arrival. This is rather different from the tie strength theory, where closeness is coupled with the duration of the relationship. Usually, closeness is not defined by the duration of the relationship. It is different because of the way in which it is defined by transnationality. Closeness and duration can each be a separate factor giving a meaning on its own. Although closeness denote both geographical difference and emotional intensity, closeness here is emotional intensity. In other words, a relationship which is far away, like an old friend, can be close as well. Closeness can become an important aspect with a person met over a weekend or after spending a week together (so closeness is not always correlated directly to the duration of the relationship). In this situation, the closeness factor comes from sharing the same situation and facing the same problems as another (here homophily playing a different role). The difficulties faced at the beginning, or experiences shared together, could also account for closeness in a relationship, as the circumstances is not currently shared by others. This occurrence may be due to the fact that others do not necessarily understand the situation, and they could be old friends or family. So, aptly, closeness can be defined as dealing with the same situation/problem. For example, having the same enemy could bring two people closer. A good example is a hospital scenario where the parents of hospitalised children befriend each other and become close through the different phases of the treatment and information shared among themselves, which they would not share with others like family or old friends. Or in the case of international students, students might find it difficult to be straightforward among local students, due to difficulty in understanding, and it could be that another student (from the same background) breaks the difference in terms of culture.

At the network level, this effect was abated with the simultaneous examination of other relational characteristics. The main structural aspects such as density or size do not play a vital role in predicting support multiplexity. When I studied the network effect on social support by considering only network aggregate measures and not relational properties, I noticed that network size played a prominent role. Although more people in the network might be synonymous with increased support, this is not reliable, as structure depends on other dimensions like density as well. This can be best illustrated by considering thirty people in a classroom, and how it is likely that only four students end up receiving support. Lots of people in the network means variety, which in turn leads to a huge probability of matching or sharing the situation in getting support from someone in that network. Taking into consideration the other structural dimensions, this facilitates the process more quickly. If a group is small, the triad effect is different. For example, in the case of a happy-go-lucky type of friendship the triad would function adequately, but there are chances of having a constraint in the relationship shared among the three if the tension is quite strong between any two of the three individuals. It can be reflected that if there are a lot of people in the network (i.e. larger networks), there are more opportunities to seek and receive support as well.

It is hypothesised that an isolate might provide support, but on the other hand there might be no more flow of support if they cease to provide support. While this is more static, the support flow through different members of the network who are well connected to each other tends to be dynamic, in the sense that there is some kind of communication flow even if the support flow stops from a particular person. For instance, imagine a family setup with the son having difficulty in accessing support from his father. If other members of the family recognise this constraint, then they might negotiate and resolve the issue as they are in the same situation. There is a dynamic flow of information between network members which makes the communication flow dynamic and ongoing. This kind of flow works only when the members of the network know each other quite well. It could also be related to a village community offering someone help in their studies. In addition to the size, support cohesion and transitivity might have a much greater influence.

In contrast to the network level, degree—which is the number of ties an alter has in the network—influenced the number of support dimensions received from their network members at the relational level. Thus, the higher the number of ties an alter has in a network, the higher the multistranded support received. The higher number of tie connections suggests a higher potential for network activity which is essential to the reception of multistranded support as compared to a large network with fewer tie connections where communication may be dormant. Apart from this, the relational constituents such as role relationships and geographical location shed more light on how the multistranded support exchange takes place for support received in addition to media factors, which is the sole relational constituent predicting multistranded support given. Proximity reflects that it does not relate to duration; people such as university students or roommates with whom everyday life and daily affairs are shared might have an influence.

Proximity could be one factor (but not the only factor) in being close to someone; in other words, not all flatmates, colleagues, or schoolmates are friends. Here, the situation defines closeness and not duration. Usually, problems arising from mundane life situations cannot always be handled by family when they are living far away. Their help comes in handy when support is sought during emotional situations, and when sharing thoughts in virtual private spaces in WhatsApp group chats, or having a phone conversation with a friend abroad. This is why multistranded support is not pronounced among family, which now makes sense. The limited involvement of close kin could differentiate between crisis, routine, and ritual care (Baldassar 2007) but there is also the point that international study abroad can be motivated by a desire to be independent of family; to have a rite of passage into adulthood.

While friends and vicinity ties supply multistranded support to the student, the student tends to supply multistranded support to other role relationships. Friendship relationships are important in networks of students, especially when they are abroad. The bubble effect of international students on campus is an unintended effect of policies/services that need a formal/informal curriculum to foster interaction with local students. Social networking sites and instant messaging did not contribute as much as the other media: other factors, that is, media profiles, predict more support than the neoteric factor. Established media, comprising primarily email and platforms like Skype, are notable for support received: it depends on the closeness of the relationship but does not necessarily require that they are from the same neighbourhood or city. Although face-to-face interactions play a huge part in such situations, they are not always good, as in the case of a bad neighbour. The descriptives explain why national ties do not really have an influence on networks' support provision. Each tie has a specialised purpose or use that it relates to, but cannot provide everything, for example, transnational ties cannot be helpful when language problems are encountered or for meeting basic needs like buying a ticket in a new country, unless the other person has been in the same setting or situation before.

The reach of receiving support also depends on the other end: how a more communicative person can be helped or may seek more support, or also having more transnational ties in the sense of reaching out and making friends in other countries also accounts for it. One possible reason is that an extroverted person has more transnational ties, or even more ties in general, and an introvert may not know many people. The behaviour of the person also plays an essential role in defining the experiences and relationships they hold. This question might influence the context and use of media. Building a relationship via face-to-face interaction is one stage in the whole process of having a relationship. At the same time, for support given by the student, it is pragmatic that the student might know the person well in advance, and may provide help in an exchange that takes place primarily through classic media.

6.5 Summary

Following the analysis and discussion, it is noteworthy that the delivery of social support to the international student, or received from the international student, depends on the social structure in which an individual or a relationship is embedded. It is important that all dyadic relations are interpreted in the light of the dyadic partners and additional relations with other network members (Hall and Wellman 1985). This internal view of social support considers the following properties of both relationships: media use and frequency; normative context and geographical location accounting for transnationalism; and structural properties (size, density, alter degree, and emotional intensity) of personal networks of international students.

All things considered, not all the characteristics observed show a significant effect when it comes to the structural level of personal networks. For example, the number of people in the student's network does not have any influence on receiving and giving multistranded support. This indicates that the size of personal networks only explains variations in particular types of support in the context of international students. Except for closeness at the structural level, in the context of international students more relational characteristics predict multistranded support received. As for support given, it is predicted by a combination of individualistic, network, and relational variables.

I assumed that highly dense networks had a greater probability of predicting multistranded support when combined with relational characteristics, despite its insignificance at the network level. But it is noted that density or interconnectedness was not positively associated with support, giving an exiguous chance that quality might cancel out quantity as indicated in the East York study (Wellman 1979). This prevailed over the finding of degree, number of connections of each network member, for multistranded support received. Although at the relational level, density is positively correlated to the emotional (r = 0.05) and instrumental (r = 0.05) support dimensions received at the 0.05 level and the emotional (r = 0.27), instrumental (r = 0.15), informational (r = 0.22), and social companionship (r = 0.21) support given at a 0.001 significance level, it is not a great predictor when combined with other aspects of networks.

Every single dimension of support had closeness as a strong predictor for social support given at network level. At the relational level, considering the network characteristics as well, it was found that the stronger the relationship, the higher the probability for multistranded support to be given as well as received. This proves that strong networks facilitate support multiplexity. This finding is in harmony with network studies of three decades ago: The first East York study (Wellman 1979), Fischer (1982) California study, and Burt (1982) US national analysis.

Strong ties, synonymous to very close ties, comprise transnational, national, and household ties. Comparing the means at the relational level, ties pertaining to certain geographical regions serve particular purposes. The effects of the structural aspects of personal networks are not particularly consistent with the theoretical assumptions. The characteristics of closeness and duration have the theoretical direction, as the students spend rather a lot of time with people who are closer, sharing the same time slot, thus more support occurs.

I proposed that co-presence is necessary for the provision of multistranded support. This in turn states that relationships in the same space/context as the student tends to facilitate multistranded support provision. The substantial supportiveness of hefty networks might be conspicuous in its substance with not only people readily available and given to be supportive, but also the student being at people's disposal for providing support to their networks. In the data, there was a predominance amongst friends in all categories of geographical dispersion except for the regional ties category. The proportion of friends in an average network is 43 per cent. The prevalence of kinship ties such as cousins, siblings, relatives, and parents living in another country shows that the family is widely spread across the globe, in their respective home country or another country. Spouses mainly shared the same household, giving the assumption that, along with their friends, it is more likely that they receive more support and different dimensions of support from people who do not live far away. Wellman and Wortley (1990) report that strong friendship ties are the essential sources of companionship. Friends and people sharing the same precincts, that is, vicinity relationships, seem to provide multistranded support in the context of international students with friends showing higher degree of influence (section

Multilevel Model of Support-Support Received in Appendix A). This is palpable in the way that these relationships provide support in an easily attainable manner.

Regardless of the high proportion of local ties, transnational ties have a standing for carrying out certain functions. Although non-transnational ties have easier access, transnational relationships are accessible, transforming the traditional way of being co-present. As seen in the descriptive section, transnational ties comprise mainly kinship ties (parents, relatives, and siblings) and friends, who fall under the category of being very close. It is widely known in the literature that kinship ties typically withstand long-distance relationships and maintain contact because of the tightly packed structure of the network and certain function (Webber 1964; Wellman and Tindall 1993).

There is negative effect for transnational as well as non-transnational ties except for regional ties related to multistranded support received. There is no influence of geographical location in terms of multistranded support given. This is in contradiction to the statement that the traditional way of being co-present facilitates more support. The dissenting effect of geographical dispersion for support received (local, national, and transnational in comparison to household ties) does not necessarily indicate that people living in those respective areas do not provide support. It means that they tend to supply uniplex support serving a single purpose and not a combination of different types of support. Contact frequency, which is usually coupled with distance, is also evident through the media factors predicting support. It is predicted in factor form that multistranded support is received through established media (email and other platforms like Skype) and given through classic media (face-to face, phone calls, and texting).

Note

1. The logistic regression of 0 (whether it is uniplex or specialised) and 1 (multistranded, receiving or giving more than one type of support) were considered. Due to missing data, the subsequent models were based on 224 cases on a structural level (networks) and 1101 cases on a relationship level (ties).

References

Antonucci, T. C., Fuhrer, R., & Dartigues, J. F. (1997). Social relations and depressive symptomatology in a sample of community-dwelling French older adults. *Psychology and Aging, 12*(1), 189.

Baldassar, L. (2007). Transnational families and the provision of moral and emotional support: The relationship between truth and distance. *Identities: Global Studies in Culture and Power, 14*(4), 385–409.

Barnes, J. A. (1972). *Social networks* (Vol. 26). Addison-Wesley Publishing Company.

Burt, R. S. (1982). *Toward a structural theory of action: Network models of social structure, perception, and action*. Academic Press.

Carrasco, J. A., & Miller, E. J. (2006). Exploring the propensity to perform social activities: A social network approach. *Transportation, 33*(5), 463–480.

Coleman, J. S. (1988). Social capital in the creation of human capital. *American Journal of Sociology, 94*, S95–S120.

Fischer, C. S. (1982). *To dwell among friends: Personal networks in town and city*. University of Chicago Press.

Gluckman, M. (1955). *The judicial process among the Barotse of Northern Rhodesia*. Manchester, UK: Manchester University Press.

Granovetter, M. S. (1977). The strength of weak ties. In *Social networks* (pp. 347–367). New York: Academic Press.

Grossetti, M. (2007). Are French networks different? *Social Networks, 29*(3), 391–404.

Hall, A., & Wellman, B. (1985). Social networks and social support. In S. Cohen & L. Syme (Eds.), *Social support and health*. New York: Academic Press.

Kapferer, B. (1969). Norms and the manipulation of relationships in a work context. In J. C. Mitchell (Ed.), *Social networks in urban situations: Analyses of personal relationships in Central African Towns* (pp. 181–244). Manchester, UK: Manchester University Press.

Marsden, P. V., & Campbell, K. E. (1984). Measuring tie strength. *Social Forces, 63*(2), 482–501.

Mitchell, J. C. (1969). The concept and use of social networks. In J. C. Mitchell (Ed.), *Social networks in urban situations: Analyses of personal relationships in Central African Towns* (pp. 1–50). Manchester, UK: Manchester University Press.

Offer, S., & Fischer, C. S. (2018). Difficult people: Who is perceived to be demanding in personal networks and why are they there? *American Sociological Review, 83*(1), 111–142.

Quan-Haase, A., & Wellman, B. (2006). Hyperconnected net work: Computer-mediated community in a high-tech organization. In C. C. Heckscher & P. S. Adler (Eds.), *The firm as a collaborative community: Reconstructing trust in the knowledge economy* (pp. 281–333). New York, NY: Oxford University Press.

Skvoretz, J., & Agneessens, F. (2007). Reciprocity, multiplexity, and exchange: Measures. *Quality & Quantity, 41*(3), 341–357.

Verbrugge, L. M. (1979). Multiplexity in adult friendships. *Social Forces, 57*(4), 1286–1309.

Webber, M. M. (1964). *The urban place and the nonplace urban realm*. University of Pennsylvania Press.

Wellman, B. (1979). The community question: The intimate networks of East Yorkers. *American Journal of Sociology, 84*(5), 1201–1231.

Wellman, B. (1988a). The community question re-evaluated. In M. P. Smith (Ed.), *Power, community and the city* (pp. 81–107). New Brunswick, NJ: Transaction Books.

Wellman, B. (1988b). Structural analysis: From method and metaphor to theory and substance. In B. Wellman & S. D. Berkowitz (Eds.), *Social structures: A network approach* (pp. 19–61). Cambridge: Cambridge University Press.

Wellman, B., & Frank, K. (2001). Network capital in a multilevel world: Getting support from personal communities. In N. Lin, K. Cook, & R. Burt (Eds.), *Social capital: Theory and research* (pp. 233–273). Hawthorne, NY: Aldine DeGruyter.

Wellman, B., & Tindall, D. (1993). Reach out and touch some bodies: How social networks connect telephone networks. *Progress in Communication Sciences, 12*, 63–93.

Wellman, B., & Wortley, S. (1990). Different strokes from different folks: Community ties and social support. *American Journal of Sociology, 96*, 558–588.

7

Conclusion

In consideration of the fundamental idea of students' social networks entailing the numerous connections and social lives submerged within them, I explored the communication flow facilitating social support across borders. The exploration brought in various perceptions, shedding light on, as well as adding intricacy to, the media use and support provision. My interest is primarily in the relationship between co-presence and support provision, and how this link is moderated by media use and frequency, therefore I examined both at the network and relational level. Firstly, I examined how different media usage patterns are formed, and also how they help in providing social support, considering the degree of transnationality in the context of international students. Secondly, I looked at the structural and relational constituents affecting the exchange of social support.

7.1 Implications

Through my examinations I discovered different types of international students' personal networks by focusing on the structural dimensions of personal communities built on the theory of structural analysis (Wellman

R. Kanagavel, *The Social Lives of Networked Students*,
https://doi.org/10.1007/978-3-319-96199-6_7

1997). The communication process employed by students, that is, different media channels' use for engaging interpersonal relationships, combined with network contents such as tie strength, structural elements, and transnationality, produced four different typologies of student's networks. It is fascinating how the division of these networks operates through structural properties and networking patterns that are beyond the usual segregation of students' networks based on their background or location. I differentiated and explained these network patterns further by the degree of cross-border mobility, specific relationship to the origin, duration of a relationship, and context of arrival. Following this, the support exchange was considered by comparing every support dimension to assess its prevalence in terms of the students' characteristics and their social networks.

The regulation of social support has been described in the literature, both at the level of structural as well as on the relational level, based on different characteristics of personal networks. The research on migrants' personal communities by Herz (2015) takes a network approach in the context of transnational studies and social support, studying the micro-processes in cross-border personal communities and examining both the relational and structural constituents. It was found that social support tends to be regulated more on a relational level, and less on a structural level. Viry (2012), in contrast, suggests that personal networks of mobile people are rather transitive. While Herz examines the support provision at the relational level using multilevel analysis, Viry uses the network level approach. In my study both of these levels were analysed, however different methods were used to gain an overview of the support exchange taking place in the students' networks.

Ties are asymmetrically reciprocal in general, contrasting in quantity and quality such that there is seldom a stationary correspondence between what is bartered between two individuals (Kadushin 1981). This is a subjective stance towards an aspect of a relationship. Ties associate with network members indirectly as well as directly, hence the need to define them within the framework of substantial structures. Asymmetric ties and networks are alleged to circulate insufficient resources. As the resources flow in and out from the student provides a careful overview, I test support given as well as received.

As discussed throughout, every international student has their own sense of consciousness in giving as well as receiving support. This led to the perception that ties between two individuals in a network are usually asymmetric in the sorts of resources or even the quantity of resources that flow from one to the other. Nonetheless, there are also certain ties that are coherent. The breadth of social support is evidence that the flow which occurs through ties and networks involves more than material goods. These flows can include information supplies, acts of kindness, or even resources that help in connecting with other less prominent ties. In the study, there was a heterogeneous mixture of support provision spanning from a friend who is in the same city to a partner who is far away in another country.

The socialisation of new media enhances new structures of transnational connections. The technology-driven social landscape somehow constructs new ways for connecting with people. Whether it is appropriating or demarcating spaces, this eventually leads to an integrated environment for different types of media. The boundaries in the mediated world have been blurred now that technology seemingly has no limits. Communicative tools are part of the social process. Each and every medium (including face-to-face contact) has distinct features and is designed to mediate and synthesise presence. The question is whether there is a variation in the usage of personal communication media, with the presence being reinforced, or rather substituted by, the social affordances proffered by various media channels. I integrated face-to-face contact as one of the media channels in the study, emphasising the mediation of face-to-face as being similar to other platforms, and looking beyond the regular distinction between online and offline worlds.

As the context of the nation state, that is, emphasis on the student's host country or home country, would be too narrow for studying the interconnections created through transnational transactions and exchanges, social network analysis enabled enquiry into practices and processes both within and across nation-states. Network analysis allows transnationality to be studied through relationships between actors, enabling the investigation of social structures which expand nation-state frameworks. The analysis of relations can be used to draw conclusions on a structural level of a kind that has only been focused upon occasionally in research on transnationality (Dahinden 2005, 2009). This form of transnational communication is comprehensible with Portes' (1994) characterisation of transnational lives as established by cross-border social relations which are consistent and maintained. These various outlooks reveal that there are diverse ways in which displacement from social interactions with the country of origin can influence an individual's sense of the social world. The relationships nurtured and their interrelation within the networks analysed bought forth the following implications.

Transnational Ties Are an Integral Part of the Flow of Support

Transnationalism as a concept has been paired with assimilation and migration, and in recent times with the topic of social support. The social structures in the networks of the students explained the process of support flow in detail, as well as activities accounting for transnationalism. In the study of Latin American immigrants in the US, Guarnizo et al. (2003) use transnational political participation for evaluating assimilation behaviour. The reverse strategy of considering acculturation or remittances as an effect and modelling it with a host of explanatory predictors including transnationalism and assimilation practices is utilised by Vacca (2013) to explain the system of assimilation or adaptation of transnational migrants in Europe. A network study among German migrants in Great Britain (Herz 2015) uses the concept of transnationalism for predicting the provision of social support. I follow the strategy whereby the transnationality is regarded as a compositional network measure to predict social support. To study the network effects, the networks themselves were employed to predict support outcomes.

The transnationality of the relationship can conceivably be a situation of both more and less social support. Intangible support such as emotional support is more likely mediated by transnational relationships at the network as well as relational level. Previous transnational studies often overemphasise mobility of persons and tend to neglect diversity, dynamic, and subjective perception. The transnational family is a symptom of our increasingly globalised lives, which take place across borders. The very idea of the transnational family implies dynamics and change; at the same time it is also implanted in unwavering structures that influence the experiences of network members.

Considering the aspect of transnationality of international students' personal networks (measured by the share of transnational relations), it is noticed that a higher proportion of transnational relations increases the probability that relationships provide emotional support. It is noteworthy to recall that nearly three quarters of the respondents (75 per cent) have at least one transnational relationship in their networks. At the relational level, it is observed that there is support multiplexity when a higher number of transnational ties is contacted through *classic media* (face-to-face contact, phone calls, and written text).

Co-Presence Is Not Influenced by the Aspect of Geographical Distance

Earlier mobility influences the contacts of the respondents to be widespread, and networks might consist of ties dispersed over different areas or concentrated in geographical areas (Viry 2012). In my study, half of the students have been abroad before, which might influence the proportion of transnational ties in their networks. This kind of dispersion ultimately roots back to not necessarily the place of origin, but different places where the international student has lived or where the members of their network have moved to. Not every student has the chance of experiencing this kind of mobility—this is totally dependent on the individual's skills, efforts, and external factors such as communication technologies and ease of transportation, which help in maintaining the resources in their respective networks.

The majority of the relationships studied experience face-to-face mediation with the student. However, when compared to household ties, other ties are less likely to be mediated often. This does not necessarily stand as an impediment to support exchange or even to having influence over one another. There is an increased frequency of texting and using other platforms like Skype for mediation of both transnational and non-transnational ties. Although there is an exclusivity in terms of few media channels used for transnational and non-transnational ties separately, this finding also reiterates that the gap of geographical distance is bridged through different media channels.

In addition to increased contact, Hampton and Wellman (2001) discern that being wired increased support interchanged with the most far-flung social ties. They also see that these network members are not that suitable for exchanging tangible goods and services due to the lack of easy physical access. Connections abroad, that is, transnational ties, not only make up the second largest proportion (next to local ties) and a relevant part in terms of the student's affective engagement, but they can be very central in personal networks as well. They might turn out to be important contacts, in that they know many of the other contacts in the network and facilitate the flow. Previous research on transnationality has shown that transnational relationships are especially favourable for emotional situations, and to a lesser degree for instrumental help or spending leisure time providing social companionship (Herz 2015).

Although it is observed in the study that more transnational ties in the students' networks facilitate more emotional support exchange, I found that media channels do facilitate other forms of transnational social support when I looked at media use and frequency controlling students' demographic information and network properties. It is noticed that instrumental support is provided by transnational ties through letters and text messages and given by the student to their transnational ties through Skype. This indicates that there is a change in mediation of social ties in the current media landscape. There are various elements of instrumental support including material support that can be transferred over distance through different mediums. It can be argued that transnational ties indirectly influence the flow of support. For example, a friend of an international student who is living abroad might help the student by connecting with their friends who are living in the student's host country. These friends in turn might help the international student to get settled in the new place.

Media Variation of Use and Frequency Depends Largely on the Network Structure

Structural dimensions contribute greatly to the understanding of individual behaviour patterns pertaining to the type and frequency of media use. Despite the increased interest most studies have in focusing on a single media tool, I chose eight media channels (face-to-face contact, letters, phone, text, email, social networking sites, IM, and other platforms like Skype) which are primarily used among international students. Despite being personal, sharing in these networks has been heavily increased with different parts of the social structure intersecting in the ego at the very centre (Chua et al. 2011). This conception can be very well applied to the media used to maintain contact with the relationships in the network. Coming to frequency of contact, the frequency of interaction between the international student and the members of the student network can be described depending on the context of the social environment. According to Homans (1961), frequent interactions reinforce common values, increase mutual awareness of needs, alleviate feelings of loneliness, and facilitate the provision of aid. It is a basic assumption that social relations as constituents of personal communities are limited to geographical proximity or distance. When it comes to the maintenance of networks, Wellman and Wortley (1990) claim that a high interaction density also promotes the provision of social support. The frequency also varies according to the context of the relationship.

I generated factors, that is, the media profiles (classic, neoteric, and established media) to reduce the eight media channel use and frequency into meaning dimensions that capture the variability of media use and frequency. For example, contact via face-to-face, phone calls, and text are used so interchangeably with the same relationships that they form a separate entity called a *classic media* profile. When the media profiles were bound together with transnationality and other structural elements, four different media patterns emerged among international students' networks. Although students belonging to each network type used their preferred media channels, networking patterns cannot be categorised in that way as every international student have their own way of connecting with people in their network. This is where I used the particularity score proposed by Hogan (2009) which determines the networking pattern for every arrangement in a student's network.

Based on this particularity score, it was divulged that media use and frequency varies a lot when there are many and various people in the network to connect. In contrast, there is less dissimilarity in the choice of media used and the frequency at which it is used when relationships are tightly packed and interrelated. Perhaps it might also be the case that there is no variation and similar media are used at regular intervals to connect with a particular group of friends. This can be well demonstrated by WhatsApp group chats where the group members know each other quite well, sharing their past and friendship while being in the same setting.

Established Media and Classic Media Facilitate More Support Received and Given

Today new media plays an essential role in students' lives and there is a demand for more of it: due to the ease of its use, there are now more expectations to be fulfilled for the student which allow them to connect with network members. Rizvi (2005) highlights the significance of transnational communication and indicates that the participants are in touch almost daily with friends and family through telephone and email. Here in the study, daily communication takes place among international students mostly through social media and platforms like Skype. This is perhaps due to the proliferation of new technologies since Rizvi's study, which took place in 2005.

Although social media platforms as such are supposed to play a small yet positive role when it comes to relationships (Tufekci and Wilson 2012), neoteric media, which are mainly composed of social media, had no influence on the prediction of multistranded support. Another notable finding is that there is no effect on support given at the relational level in terms of having face-to-face contact, while all the other media channels in one way or another predict different dimensions of support. On the other hand, instrumental support and social companionship support dimensions received do influence the frequency of meeting someone in person.

When examining the dyadic level, it was found that the *established media* profile (email and other platforms like Skype) influences the multistranded support received and *classic media* (face-to-face contact, phone calls and text) influences the multistranded support given. This can be illustrated more comprehensively through the prediction of frequency of media channels. Email, one of the media channels belonging to the *established media* profile, is mainly used for receiving three kinds of support, namely emotional, instrumental and informational, from the members of networks. At the same time, texting from a mobile phone (*classic media*) is used to give back multistranded support (emotional, informational and social companionship) to the network members.

Tie Strength Acts as a Prominent Factor

While considering closeness, there is a difference in the evaluation of the tie shared between ego and alter and between two alters in the network. Usually when eliciting the relationship between ego and alter, the measure of the strength is evaluated by the extent of closeness. The interaction between students and their network members plays a role in the determination of the intensity of the tie strength, as it involves one or both people's efforts to maintain the tie. Rather than considering very close persons as those with whom one regularly interacts, I use the words "regularly keep in touch with". Here it does not really mean that the contact is regular, but it does denote that the student shares a mutual interest in maintaining contact. It also frames the kind of contact as being concerned towards mutual affection.

There is a huge difference in keeping in touch and regularly interacting. A person who is working with a colleague may often interact in terms of a task or job that has to be completed. However, keeping in touch with a colleague who is not really near or working in the same office is what matters. This is where the use of media and physical proximity play a role. Some factors may appear to be very explicit, but in-depth analysis provides more vivid ideas regarding the link between media use and tie strength. Marsden and Campbell's (1984) disapproval of contact frequency as a degree of tie strength coincides with the above idea, as they point out that numerous individuals are in frequent contact because of shared space or location. This does not really exclude these persons from a personal network. But it is not a feature which is sufficient when talking about tie strength. There are various outlooks, and here in the study I mainly focus on everyday life where the student has their own pattern of networking. In former times, when networking meant only having a network with neighbours, it was almost compulsory to stick with the people around them due to the proximity factor and limited options. This enhanced more homogeneous relationships by the sharing of mutual interests. This is the paradox of whether homogeneity necessarily produces strong ties.

Stronger ties may not necessitate face-to-face contact much, just like how you can go without seeing important members in the network and still feel connected or sustain a long-distance relationship. Moreover, as ties with relatives tend to be densely knit while friendship ties tend to be more discrete relationships, relations with kin may survive greater distances than relations with friends (Wellman and Wortley 1990). Closeness necessitates trust; trust in turn requires a time period. This kind of intimacy might be necessary for sharing of personal matters, while providing aid or imparting information does not necessarily take place between intimate people. Although half of the ties are very close, and an average network consists of a small number of support providers, the threshold of being close is important when it comes to giving more dimensions of support. Apart from the support aspect, I see that the prediction of media use is also largely dependent on socio-emotional intensity, that is, closeness.

7.2 Mobility and Its Effects

Sojourns to other countries, especially for studying abroad, are increasingly common. The opportunities provided by universities to study abroad and the presence of international students in universities worldwide offers a wide range of benefits not only to the international students themselves but also to people and the culture in the local communities. At the same time it also provides a lot of challenges. At university level, one of the most important challenges faced involves adequate provision of social support for international students. At the very beginning, an international student advisor might handle the task of helping the students adapt to their new surroundings through events and orientation programmes. The organisation of orientation programmes often aims to introduce new international students to their institutions. These advisors provide assistance in finding accommodation and have the responsibility of preparing cross-cultural programmes to enable students to learn more about the host country's culture. While programmes such as tandem partnership, national team outings, recreational club memberships, and weekend travels facilitate easy integration into the school and settings, students are exposed to numerous other events and communities through their social circles. At the individual level it also depends on the choices made by the international students to seek and receive social support.

Adjusting to new life in a different country can be demanding and can require significant effort. Students need to not only maintain and expand their social networks, but also continuously seek information about their new environment until it becomes familiar. The social lives of the students involve new relationships in the host country that are made and nurtured at the same time as maintaining old relationships from elsewhere. I agree that geographical distance has an influence on social relationships in general. Although international students' lives are in focus, I reflect upon another form of mobility to provide a comparative reference. In other words, if we would take another form of mobility, say expatriates, would the findings be so different? I conducted a small-scale study among 58 expatriates using a version of the *IntStudLink* survey that was modified and shortened so that it was appropriate for the expatriate group. International expatriates experience mobility differently than international students, which can be reflected in the structure of networks and in support exchanges.

Looking at the demographic information, 46 per cent of the expatriates who lived in Asia (there was a predominance of respondents in Singapore, Bangkok, and Hong Kong) were from Europe, whereas the remaining expatriates in the study who lived in US (28 per cent), UK (19 per cent) and Germany (seven per cent) were mainly from Asian countries. The average duration of stay in their respective countries is 2.4 years.

The average age of the expatriates was 31.22 years. Expatriate's networks comprise nearly 64 per cent of local ties and only 23 per cent of transnational ties—this might be due to the length of the time period in the host country. In agreement with studies on neighbourhood and communities (Gabriel and Bowling 2004; Attree et al. 2011), the personal relationships constructed and fostered through community activities seem to contribute to expats' social lives. The composition of important role relationships is as follows: 66 per cent of friends, 19 per cent spouses, eight per cent of vicinity ties and seven per cent of family.

Controlling for expatriates' demographics and network data, I found that the more local the expatriates' networks are, the more support they receive from their network members. While research shows transnational communities generated by mobility depend on family ties (Theodore and Martin 2007), my finding on expats' networks, by contrast, proves that they are much more dependent on local ties comprising friends and colleagues than transnational ties when it comes to seeking social support. When I studied reciprocity of support, it can be seen that social companionship and emotional support are given equally to both transnational and local ties. *Classic media* (comprising face-to-face, phone, and text) was used to receive support whereas neoteric media was used by the students to give support.

Although transnational ties play an imperative role in international students' networks, it is noticed that local relationships get an equivalent share of ties (Chap. 2). This is in contrast to the research findings on international students at a UK university (Montgomery 2010) where it is found that many of them fail to establish meaningful local friendships. However, the research also shows that most international students are open to new experiences and undergo significant personal transformations during their sojourn abroad.

When asked about the immediate plan after their studies, 40 per cent of the international students plan to return to their home country. It might be that they want to go back to their family or that they are well-rooted in their home country that there is a necessity to return. Twenty-nine per cent of respondents plan to stay in their current country of residence and nearly 27 per cent intend to move to another country. This could relate to the economic conditions of that country or situation faced by the student. On the other hand, the plan to move to another country could be because of the insatiable quest for exploration or even circumstances which are not favourable in both their country of residence and home country.

Apart from ties abroad, there is no prevalence of ties at regional or national level in terms of geographical distance. The prominence of ties in the same city or neighbourhood in a student's and expatriate's network, and no proper connections in other areas spread across the residing country, reminds me of the idea of "bilocalism" proposed by Lucassen (2006) and Waldinger (2010). In most cases, transnationalism is the maintenance of ties between two local communities and does not actually relate to the national level.

7.3 Strengths and Limitations

The underlying theme of the book—to study the social lives of the students—was accomplished using a network approach. Egocentric network analysis as an analytical tool seemed to be appropriate for a study on social support exchange and media use taking place between relationships belonging to international students' networks. It facilitated the evaluation of the theoretical framework and the development of instruments accessing the students' networks.

Considering the interdependence between frequency of contact and distance, media tools are employed accordingly so that it covers most of the widely used personal communication media including in-person contact. The study by Mok and Wellman (2007) examined the changing role of distance in influencing face-to-face and phone contact between the 1970s and the 2000s (the pre- and post-internet age). They inspected the impact of distance on the members of a personal network. At that time, email and phone were the main media used, so they looked at whether these media outputs were disparate according to the distance; this is a question of the location of the target group. The target group of the East York study (Wellman 1979) were concentrated in one locality all the time, whereas the students here are drawn from different parts of the world.

Communication tools have been spreading rapidly, especially among the younger population. I addressed some of the media dimensions primarily used, to the best of my knowledge, in today's mobile world. However, further media channels can be chosen and analysed. Previous research in the field of media studies hold face-to-face interactions in higher regard compared to any other form of communication (Song 2009). I contend that face-to face interactions are very much part of mediated interactions. Although these interactions have steadily changed the social landscape as the internet has become entrenched in our daily lives, the discussions revolve around the nature of the community rather than focusing on the technology advancement and how it affects social life. Future research on the issues of how a variety of new technologies are used to sustain or change personal relationships can incorporate the concept and the framework behind the analysis to study groups with other demographics.

The highlight of the study is the geographical distribution of the international students in terms of both country of residence as well as country of origin. This not only overcomes the idea of "methodological nationalism", that is, the focus on one particular country, but also offers a new perspective for consideration of a sample for transnational studies in general. Although the results are based on a culturally and linguistically diverse population of students, there is a high probability of student participation in Europe as the survey distribution is concentrated in this region. It is important to heed this diversity in the development of field work. I compare the characteristics of students in the self-selective sample of the study with the characteristics of students in the OECD study on international study mobility (Sect. 1.5 in Chap. 1) to show how the findings are generalised to a broader population.

The closeness factor seems to play a vital role in personal communities of international students with regard to support exchange. This might be because of their tendency to contact the close ties more often as demonstrated in the prediction of frequency of media use. I presume that the course of events might change with respect to support circulation if the sample included weak ties as well. When weak ties are incorporated, there is a chance of a larger degree of transnationality and less media multiplexity. Furthermore, the questions used for elicitation also determine the type of ties elicited.

Although certain assumptions of this research can be considered widely, it must be kept in mind that the study is target-group specific. The research context and the sample chosen might not be representative of the whole population of international students. To assess the magnitude of the sampling, the survey participants were asked at the end of the questionnaire about how they had become aware of the study. Over one third of the respondents, that is, 91 (40.9 per cent) of the 222 respondents became aware of the survey by receiving an email invitation from their respective universities. The next major distribution was through my personal invitations (25.2 per cent) and through forwarding of the survey requested by another colleague/friend (27.4 per cent). Social networking sites contributed greatly as well, where 28 respondents (12.6 per cent) came to know about the survey via Facebook and nine respondents in particular mentioned Reddit to be the source. Although snowball sampling method was selected for the investigation, it is estimated only around 25 per cent of the respondents were recruited through another participant. This is expedient as the prerequisite for a network study is that there should be no overlap between members in the networks considered for analysis.

It might be constructive to extend the research and undertake longitudinal studies incorporating a broader range of students with respect to origin and destination. This would enable the analysis of these networks that tend to change over time, allowing the estimation of more models of the effect of changes in network structure on relationships among peer groups and communication flow within the networks. In spite of the fact that the present network data encompassing ties spanning across borders might pose methodological challenges, more network features like centrality might be incorporated, which may contribute more to the provision of support.

7.4 "Digital" Social Transformation?

Sharing a relationship with someone and nurturing it through the years, dealing with external impediments like distance that come along with it, is an exciting experience in itself. With technologies and the social affordances they offer, a complicated scenario is made a little simpler. While some manage it with ease, some have difficulties as it involves investment of time and energy to fulfil a need. Nowadays, media are embedded in everyday life especially in the case of international students. The World Unplugged[1] project demonstrates how media, be it Instagramming or 280 character-limits of news, turns out to be essential and pervasive in the case of students, so is a good exemplar for this. Although there are plenty of chances to discuss the part played by digital-age technologies in the transformations of personal relationships, somehow the route changed with the distinction between real and online worlds so that addressing the transformations was postponed.

I see the existence of the diversity of mobile lives and points of intersection between expatriates and students. The concept of globalisation is nurtured by the mediated communication, with no hindrance to local or distant contacts. The affordances of the internet have not only increased social interactions but have also helped in providing easier and cheap communication, even when the person is living oceans away.

New media is changing the social landscape as well as our mediated interactions (Baym 2015). On an average day, meeting my friends or colleagues at the university, socialising, and having lunch with them is part and parcel of my everyday life. At the same time, talking to my dad through SmartVoip or sending a text through WhatsApp to a friend in Holland is also part of my daily life.

In migrant transnationalism studies, social change is usually measured through circumstances prevailing in different settings which have an effect on the values and practices of a social organization (Vertovec 2009). He alludes to other theorists describing global connectivity as "global-enduring structural shifts in social political and economic organization" and indicates those shifts as various kinds of transformation. I presume that the best approach is not either/or but rather asking how the use of communication technologies is transforming the way we support care (including in proximate settings) and our ability to receive or give support across distance.

It is revealed that support received or given with co-presence is socially constructed in specific contexts in both international students' and expatriates' networks. In general, all of us want attention, love, and support only from our personally-defined support network and not from individuals external to it. We desire support which is reciprocal in nature where the support being offered is from an individual to whom we are receptive. So, whether a friend or family member's support is perceived as co-present depends on the individual's experience of that support. To put this another way, objectively, all the forms of support described have the potential to be delivered in multiple ways. However, they are experienced and defined very differently.

Although support circulation does not presuppose physical co-presence, it remains an empirical question as to the way in which technologies passing on support replace proximity-based care practices (Baldassar and Merla 2013). All things considered, it is also the site through which communication takes place and undergoes a transformation. This acts as a catalyst for someone to be more communicative, more supportive, or even more receptive, depending on the location and selection of the resources. The phatic function, the SMS or email and the like, which are also expressions of care, is one of the novel ways of creating the support function. At the same time, there is also an increased expectation to be in touch with, or visit, our connections.

We live in an era where we access and use advanced technologies to connect with people. As our lives are entangled with these innovations in today's technology, it is important to acknowledge the digital forms of support exchange. New forms of support/co-presence present a rich scenario, along with structural and relational explanations of social phenomena. The research on students' networks in this book is not conclusive, but an ongoing discussion on how support flow is regulated from localised areas to long-distance connections through new forms of communication. While Holmes (2002) proposes that it involves either commute or communication for exchange to take place in a community, I suggest that it can be both ways. The subsumption of these activities in the system of mediated connections emerges out of engaging tendencies to sign out or stay connected, to break free or to remain tethered.

Note

1. A global media study conducted by the University of Maryland College Park in 2010 on nearly 1000 students in ten countries on five continents (Chile, China, Slovakia, Mexico, Lebanon, UK, Argentina, US, and Uganda) who refrained from using all media for 24 hours. The students admitted that it was rather difficult to survive without any kind of media for a day.

References

Attree, P., French, B., Milton, B., Povall, S., Whitehead, M., & Popay, J. (2011). The experience of community engagement for individuals: A rapid review of evidence. *Health & Social Care in the Community, 19*(3), 250–260.

Baldassar, L., & Merla, L. (Eds.). (2013). *Transnational families, migration and the circulation of care: Understanding mobility and absence in family life* (Vol. 29). Routledge.

Baym, N. K. (2015). *Personal connections in the digital age*. John Wiley & Sons.

Chua, V., Madej, J., & Wellman, B. (2011). Personal communities: The world according to me. In J. Scott & P. J. Carrington (Eds.), *The SAGE handbook of social network analysis* (pp. 101–115). Thousand Oaks, CA: Sage.

Dahinden, J. (2005). Contesting transnationalism? Lessons from the study of Albanian migration networks from former Yugoslavia. *Global Networks, 5*(2), 191–208.

Dahinden, J. (2009). Are we all transnationals now? Network transnationalism and transnational subjectivity: The differing impacts of globalization on the inhabitants of a small Swiss city. *Ethnic and Racial Studies, 32*(8), 1365–1386.

Gabriel, Z., & Bowling, A. (2004). Quality of life from the perspectives of older people. *Ageing & Society, 24*(5), 675–691.

Guarnizo, L. E., Portes, A., & Haller, W. (2003). Assimilation and transnationalism: Determinants of transnational political action among contemporary migrants. *American Journal of Sociology, 108*(6), 1211–1248.

Hampton, K., & Wellman, B. (2001). Long distance community in the network society: Contact and support beyond Netville. *American Behavioral Scientist, 45*(3), 476–495.

Herz, A. (2015). Relational constitution of social support in migrants' transnational personal communities. *Social Networks, 40*, 64–74.

Hogan, B. J. (2009). *Networking in everyday life*. Toronto, ON, Canada: University of Toronto.

Holmes, D. (2002). Virtual globalization – An introduction. In *Virtual globalization* (pp. 11–64). Routledge.

Homans, G. C. (1961). *Human behavior: Its elementary forms*. Harcourt Brace.

Kadushin, C. (1981). *Long term stress reactions: Some causes, consequences, and naturally occurring support systems*. Department of Sociology, State University of New York.

Lucassen, L. (2006). *Is transnationalism compatible with assimilation? Examples from the Western Europe since 1850*. Paper for the conference Migrants, Nations and Citizenship, CRASSH, University of Cambridge, 5–6 July.

Marsden, P. V., & Campbell, K. E. (1984). Measuring tie strength. *Social Forces, 63*(2), 482–501.

Mok, D., & Wellman, B. (2007). Did distance matter before the Internet?: Interpersonal contact and support in the 1970s. *Social Networks, 29*(3), 430–461.

Montgomery, C. (2010). *Understanding the international student experience.* Palgrave Macmillan.

Portes, A. (1994). Introduction: Immigration and its aftermath. *The International Migration Review, 28*(4), 632–639.

Rizvi, F. (2005, March). International education and the production of cosmopolitan identities. In *Transnational seminar series.*

Song, F. W. (2009). *Virtual communities: Bowling alone, online together.* Peter Lang.

Theodore, N., & Martin, N. (2007). Migrant civil society: New voices in the struggle over community development. *Journal of Urban Affairs, 29*(3), 269–287.

Tufekci, Z., & Wilson, C. (2012). Social media and the decision to participate in political protest: Observations from Tahrir Square. *Journal of Communication, 62*(2), 363–379.

Vacca, R. (2013). *Bridging across nations. The social capital of diversity, brokerage and closure in transnational migrant networks: A study on assimilation patterns in Milan and Barcelona.* Unpublished doctoral thesis, Università degli studi di Milano-Bicocca.

Vertovec, S. (2009). *Transnationalism.* London and New York: Routledge.

Viry, G. (2012). Residential mobility and the spatial dispersion of personal networks: Effects on social support. *Social Networks, 34*(1), 59–72.

Waldinger, R. (2010). Rethinking transnationalism. *Empiria. Revista de Metodología de las Ciencias Sociales, 19*, 21–38.

Wellman, B. (1979). The community question: The intimate networks of East Yorkers. *American Journal of Sociology, 84*(5), 1201–1231.

Wellman, B. (1997). Structural analysis: From method and metaphor to theory and substance. *Contemporary Studies in Sociology, 15*, 19–61.

Wellman, B., & Wortley, S. (1990). Different strokes from different folks: Community ties and social support. *American Journal of Sociology, 96*(3), 558–588.

Appendix A: Methodology

Cluster Analysis

I use the non-hierarchical clustering, which is called *k*-means, where *k* is the number of clusters, since a case or individual is ascribed to the cluster for which its distance from the cluster mean is the smallest. The main challenge in the procedure centres on finding the *k*-means. There is an initial set of means and cases which are classified based on their distances from the centres. Then, the cluster means are calculated again, using the cases that were assigned to the clusters (Table A.1). This is then repeated through iterations until permanent clusters were formed.

One of the things to be considered in cluster analysis is identifying the number of clusters. This is overcome by performing both hierarchical and non-hierarchical analysis. First, hierarchical analysis is conducted to get an idea of the number of clusters and the manner in which they combine from a dendrogram. Hierarchical clustering requires a distance/similarity matrix between all pairs of cases. This will result in a massive matrix, whereas *k*-means clustering does not require calculation of all possible distances. After this, *k*-means technique is performed where the chosen

R. Kanagavel, *The Social Lives of Networked Students*,
https://doi.org/10.1007/978-3-319-96199-6

Table A.1 Cluster centres for the standardised network properties ($N = 229$)

	Type I *Like or Follow me*	Type II *Let's meet asap :)*	Type III *FaceTime or Skype?*	Type IV *Where's the party tonight?*
Size	−0.19	−0.15	−0.66	1.89
Density	−0.43	0.03	1.26	−1.1
Transnationality	0.71	−0.81	0.23	0.24
Closeness	−0.06	−0.37	0.76	−0.59
Classic media	−0.14	0.21	0.17	−0.32
Neoteric media	0.12	0.02	0.02	−0.22
Established media	0.14	−0.21	0.46	−0.2

number of clusters is given, and the analysis is rerun. During the analysis, *k*-means clustering recurrently reallocates cases to clusters, so the same case can move from cluster to cluster. The analysis shows four different types of personal network in the context of international students.

Multilevel Model of Support

Transmissions of social support are properties of both the relations and structural dimensions of personal communities. This means that in the analysis of ego-centred network data, two levels of analysis are used: the relational level and the network level. Social relations (level 1) is the unit of analysis, which is thought to be embedded within personal networks (level 2). The dependent variable, that is, whether a relationship is specialised or multistranded (providing more than one type of support), can be explained through effects on different levels: relational or alter-level (level 1) and individual and network properties or ego-level (level 2), that is, the structural aspects of personal communities.

To answer the question of whether properties of social relations, structural properties of personal communities, and characteristics of the egos affect the provision of different kinds of social support, multilevel logistic regression analysis was applied in R. This approach is also suitable for dealing with the nested structure of the ego-centred network data. As the dependent variable was binary coded, logistic regression models were applied in which the unit of analysis was the directed tie between alter and ego, and the dependent variable was whether this tie provides multi-stranded social support (1) or not (0). A tie was counted as multistranded for the different support dimensions when more than one name generator elicited the same person in the network.

A first step towards modelling between-group variability is to let the constant or intercept vary between the networks, that is, the individuals. This reflects that some individuals tend to have, on average, higher responses of support given or received, and others tend to have lower responses. Before heading to the estimation of the models, it is quite important to check the variance with the help of an empty or null model. I started with a simple model that assesses whether there is sufficient variance between networks. As expected, the variance indicated that the consideration of multilevel models was appropriate.

Support Received

As the elemental objective of the study is to fathom the relationship between support and media, only the media factors were introduced in the first model. All of the media factors were significant in the basic model, disclosing a positive association between the property of multiplexity of support dimensions and media. The significant effect for classic and established media was at 0.001, whereas neoteric media exhibited a 0.01 level. In the second model, when the social demographics of ego and homophilous characteristics shared by the alters and ego were added, it was seen that the significance of the media factors was retained. Along with this, there was a weak positive relationship between ego gender and support received. Female students have a higher probability of receiving multistranded support than male students. There was no association between homophily and support received.

After the introduction of structural and relational characteristics in the third model, the neoteric media lost its significance. There is a strong positive significant effect in terms of emotional intensity. The closer the ties, the more likely respondents are to receive multistranded support. The longer you know a person, the less likely you are to receive multistranded support from them. This gives an assumption that family known for a long time serves a different purpose to people known for a shorter amount of time. The alter degree covariate seems to be a significant factor. The more ties the member of the network has, the more multiplex ties, which means the flow of resources through the sufficient number of ties allows access to more support received (Table A.2).

Friends and people who live in and share the same vicinity seem more likely to provide multistranded support. With regard to geographical distance, the more the local, national, or even transnational ties, the less likely someone is to receive multistranded support compared to the base category of household ties. The fourth model, which was the final one, remained the same except for the addition of established media factor after the addition of cross-level interactions. Established media, which comprises email and other platforms like Skype, was found to be significant, conveying that the higher the use and frequency of these media channels, the higher the probability of receiving multistranded support. One significant effect was noticed when the proportion of transnational ties (network level) interacted with the use of media through media factors (tie level). It can be interpreted that the higher the proportion of transnational ties contacted through classic media (face-to-face, phone calls, and text), the higher the probability of receiving multistranded support.

Support Given

The multilevel logistic regression provided a test of significance, and then reciprocal exchange of support was again examined considering the ego providing multistranded support to alters at the relational level. The significant variance intercepts in the models indicate that not all individuals give the same degree of social support within their personal networks. Methodologically, the application of the multilevel design is adequate for analysing the reciprocity of support as well.

The social support dimensions of this study encompass just the positive aspects of the support literature although constraints could be taken into consideration. The reason behind this limitation is mainly due to the

Table A.2 Random intercept models for support received

	Model 1	Model 2	Model 3	Model 4
(Intercept)	−0.75***	−1.86***	0.01***	0.04
Media profiles				
Classic	0.58***	0.55***	0.32.	−0.13
Neoteric	0.35**	0.39**	0.12	−0.05
Established	0.45***	0.51***	0.54**	0.62*
Demographics				
Ego's gender (female)		0.78.	0.62	0.61
Ego's age (mc)		0	0	0.01
Time since arrival (mc)		−0.04	−0.05	−0.05
Homophily				
Same age (±3)		0.24	−0.02	−0.02
Same gender		0.18	0.04	0.04
Same country of origin		0.11	0.04	0.04
Tie strength				
Closeness (gmc)			0.73***	0.74***
Duration (mc)			−0.03**	−0.03**
Structure				
Density			−1.5	−1.52
Size			0.02	0.02
Degree			0.44.	0.45.
Role relationships				
Partner			0.43	0.47
Family			0.65	0.21
Vicinity			0.55.	0.54.
Friend			0.65*	0.69*
Others			−0.09	−0.08
Geographical distance				
Local			−1.01**	−1.02**
Regional			−0.78	−0.77
National			−1.38*	−1.42*
Transnational			−1.16**	−1.08*
Cross level interactions				
Classic: Transnational ties				1.21*
Neoteric: Transnational ties				0.46
Established: Transnational ties				−0.19
AIC	1404	1300	1211	1212
BIC	1430	1360	1326	1342
Log Likelihood	−697	−637	−582	−579
Deviance	1394	1276	1165	1160
Num. obs.	1230	1139	1286	1101
Num. groups: egoID	277	238	224	224
Variance: egoID. (Intercept)	6.86	6.96	7.75	7.6

target group as well as the duration of their stay in their host country. Another important aspect in social support research is the reciprocity seen in the networks. The support provided to the ego was collected through the name generator elicitation process, whereas the data on the support given by the ego to their network members was collected in the last question of the name interpreter question. So, it is possible to see the support given from the ego to the alters by constructing models like the previous models explaining the support given from the alters to the ego. The binary logit multilevel regression analyses were repeated, as they were specifically designed to be used for dichotomous dependent variables. In this case, the dichotomous dependent variables were "ego provides multistranded support" (1) and "ego provides uniplex support" (0).

In the multiplex model of support given from the ego to other members of the network, history repeated itself in the first model. All of the media factors seemed to be very significant (Table A.3). In the second model, augmented with demographic variables, it was noticed that gender (being female) had a positive association at 0.05 level. There was a positive significant effect with the homophilous age and origin of alter and ego. As on average 43 per cent of the students' networks comprised friends, and university friends are likely to be a similar age, it was appropriate to choose three years as a level of magnitude for measuring homophily. So, alters three years younger or older than the ego were considered to be homophilous relations. It seems that the higher the number of homophilous relations in terms of age, the more likely they are to be not specialised ties but multistranded ties responsible for the provision of numerous kinds of support. The same country of origin had a positive significant effect, which goes back to the theory that *birds of a feather flock together* in terms of origin.

The homophilous country of origin and established media factor subsided after the addition of the relational and structural variables in the third model. Similar to the models for support received, tie strength measuring closeness seemed to be significant for support given as well. In the final model, after the introduction of cross-interactions, classic media were the most-used media through which support is given back, while the receivers who fall under the "other relationships" category tend to be close and of more or less the same age, accounting for homophily.

Table A.3 Random intercept models for support given

	Model 1	Model 2	Model 3	Model 4
(Intercept)	2.3	0.86	2.06	3.4
Media profiles				
Classic	0.47***	0.54***	0.62**	0.74*
Neoteric	0.85***	0.76***	0.53**	0.22
Established	0.46***	0.58***	0.14	0.08
Demographics				
Ego's gender (female)		0.73*	1.71*	0.6
Ego's age (mc)		0.03	0.03	0.02
Time since arrival (mc)		0.1	0.11	0.11
Homophily				
Same age (±3)		1.08***	1.10***	1.10***
Same gender		0.19	0.1	0.11
Same country of origin		0.47.	0.01	0
Tie strength				
Closeness (gmc)			1.13***	1.13***
Duration (mc)			−0.01	−0.01
Structure				
Density			0.16	0.09
Size			0.32	0.3
Degree			0.05	0.08
Role relationships				
Partner			0.81	1.15
Family			−0.11	−0.87
Vicinity			0.41	0.4
Friend			0.37	0.39
Others			−1.21	1.44.
Geographical distance				
Local			−0.24	−0.22
Regional			−0.4	−0.35
National			0.88	0.9
Transnational			0.21	0.23
Cross level interactions				
Classic: Transnational ties				−0.25
Neoteric: Transnational ties				0.83
Established: Transnational ties				0.17
AIC	1138	1035	940.5	945.8
BIC	1164	1091	1058	1084
Log Likelihood	−563.8	−506.3	−447.2	−445.9
Deviance	464.11	1013	894.5	891.8
Num. obs.	1441	1270	1231	1231
Num. groups: egoID	280	240	225	225
Variance: egoID. (Intercept)	3.81	3.94	4.61	4.55

Appendix B: *IntStudLink* Questionnaire

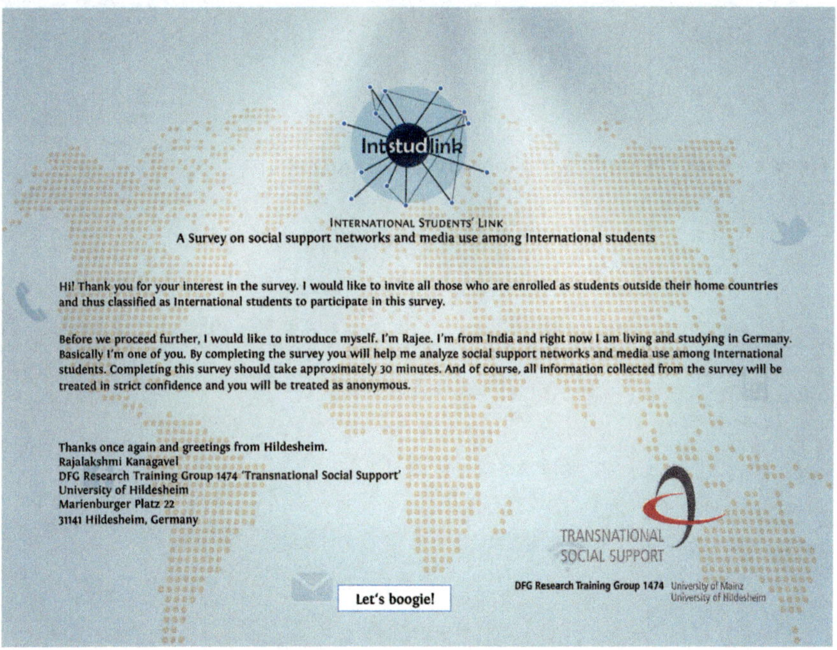

Fig. B.1 Front cover of the online survey *IntStudLink*

R. Kanagavel, *The Social Lives of Networked Students*,
https://doi.org/10.1007/978-3-319-96199-6

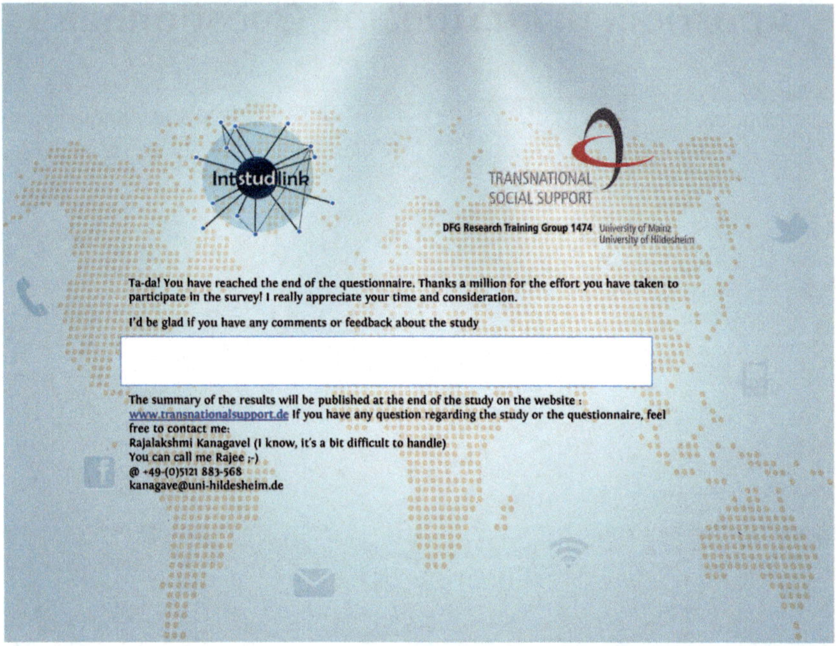

Fig. B.2 Back cover of the online survey *IntStudLink*

MOBILITY AND MOTIVES

1. In which year did you arrive in your current country of residence?

_ _ _ _

2. In which country do you currently reside?

____

3. What were the three most important reasons for your move to your country of residence? ***(Please write the reason number in the option box)***

- ☐ Most important
- ☐ Second most important
- ☐ Third most important

1. Very important and/or famous university, professor, study programme in my field
2. I got the scholarship offer
3. I would have had wider employment opportunities in my home country after graduation
4. I would have had wider employment opportunities abroad after graduation
5. I would get access to social security and benefits
6. I accompanied my partner/family
7. I liked the language of instruction
8. I liked the culture & lifestyle of the country
9. Affordable cost of tuition
10. Advice of colleagues, peers or friends
11. My home university had an agreement with this institution
12. Other reasons

4. Before coming to your current country of residence, had you lived outside of your home country, staying in one location for one month or longer?

- o Yes
- o No

5. For the two longest periods of your stay abroad please specify in which country you lived, the duration of your stay and the purpose of your stay.

Country	Year	Duration of stay	Purpose of stay
1st longest stay abroad Please write the name of the country here __________	_ _ _ _	o Less than 3 months o From 3 to 6 months o From 6 months to 1 year o From 1 to 3 years o More than 3 years	o Study-related o Employment on own o Initiative o Projects, research o assignments or internships o Accompanying partner or o Family o Vacation o I don't remember
1st longest stay abroad Please write the name of the country here __________	_ _ _ _	o Less than 3 months o From 3 to 6 months o From 6 months to 1 year o From 1 to 3 years o More than 3 years	o Study-related o Employment on own o Initiative o Projects, research o assignments or internships o Accompanying partner or o Family o Vacation o I don't remember

6. What do you plan to do as the next major step after completing your current degree? ***(You may select more than one option)***

- ☐ I plan to stay in my current country of residence
- ☐ I plan to return to my home country
- ☐ I intend to move to another country
- ☐ I don't know
- ☐ Other plans, please specify ______________

7. How long would you like to stay in your current country of residence (from now onwards)?

- o Less than 1 year
- o 1 to 2 years
- o 2 to 3 years
- o 3 to 5 years
- o More than 5 years
- o I don't know

8. To which country are you planning to move? (Please write the country)

____

9. How long would you like to stay in that country?

- o Less than 1 year
- o 1 to 2 years
- o 2 to 3 years
- o 3 to 5 years
- o More than 5 years
- o I don't know

10. What residential status do you currently hold in your current country of residence?

- o Student permit
- o Residence permit for researchers
- o Family residence permit (joining a family member)
- o Work permit
- o Permanent (settlement) residence permit
- o Citizenship of the residing country
- o I don't know
- o Other (Please name) _________

11. Do you take part in activities associated with any organizations (sports/leisure organizations, NGOs/ volunteering organizations or students networks) based in your present country of residence?

- o Yes
- o No

12. Are you a member of any association/group (not necessarily based in your present country of residence) whose members are mainly of your origin?

- o Yes
- o No

13. Are you a member of any association/group (not necessarily based in your present country of residence) whose members are mainly international students?

- o Yes
- o No

14. How often are you in contact with people in your home country?

- o Daily
- o Several times a week
- o About once a week
- o Several times a month
- o About once a month
- o Five times a year
- o Less than five times a year
- o Never

15. How often do you socialize with people from your home country in your current country of residence?

- o Daily
- o Several times a week
- o About once a week
- o Several times a month
- o About once a month
- o Five times a year
- o Less than five times a year
- o Never

16. How often do you socialize with other international people in your current country of residence?

- o Daily
- o Several times a week
- o About once a week
- o Several times a month
- o About once a month
- o Five times a year
- o Less than five times a year
- o Never

17. How often have you visited your home country since you have been in your current country of residence?

- o Daily
- o Several times a week
- o About once a week
- o Several times a month
- o About once a month
- o Five times a year
- o Less than five times a year
- o Never

MEDIA USE

18.* Which of the following do you possess? *(You can select more than one)

- ☐ Landline phone
- ☐ Mobile phone (cell phone/smartphone)
- ☐ Desktop/Laptop/Tablet

***19.* Do you have an internet connection on your mobile phone?**

- o Yes
- o No

***20.* How often do you contact people living in your current country of residence via mobile phone calls?**

- o Daily
- o Several times a week
- o About once a week
- o Several times a month
- o About once a month
- o Five times a year
- o Less than five times a year
- o Never

***21.* How often do you contact people living outside your current country of residence via mobile phone calls?**

- o Daily
- o Several times a week
- o About once a week
- o Several times a month
- o About once a month
- o Five times a year
- o Less than five times a year
- o Never

22. **How often do you contact people living in your current country of residence via text message (SMS)?**

- o Daily
- o Several times a week
- o About once a week
- o Several times a month
- o About once a month
- o Five times a year
- o Less than five times a year
- o Never

23. **How often do you contact people living outside your current country of residence via text message (SMS)?**

- o Daily
- o Several times a week
- o About once a week
- o Several times a month
- o About once a month
- o Five times a year
- o Less than five times a year
- o Never

24. **How often do you contact people living in your current country of residence via landline phone calls?**

- o Daily
- o Several times a week
- o About once a week
- o Several times a month
- o About once a month
- o Five times a year
- o Less than five times a year
- o Never

25. **How often do you contact people living outside your current country of residence via landline phone calls?**

- o Daily
- o Several times a week
- o About once a week
- o Several times a month
- o About once a month
- o Five times a year
- o Less than five times a year
- o Never

26. **Do you have an internet connection on your desktop/laptop/tablet?**

- o Yes
- o No

27. **How often do you use the internet?**

- o Daily
- o Several times a week
- o About once a week
- o Several times a month
- o About once a month
- o Five times a year
- o Less than five times a year
- o Never

28. **On an average day, how many hours do you spend on the internet? (including working hours)**

— —

29. **Do you use social platforms like Facebook, Linkedln, Youtube, Skype to contact others?**

- o Yes
- o No

30. **How frequently do you visit social networking sites?**

- o More than 5 times a day
- o 5 times a day
- o 2-4 times a day
- o Once a day
- o 3-4 times a week
- o 1-2 times a week
- o Few times a month
- o Never

31. **On how many social networking sites do you have a profile?**

— —

32. **Which site do you use most often?**

- o Facebook
- o Myspace
- o Google+
- o Flickr
- o Twitter
- o Other (Please name) ___________

SOCIAL NETWORK

The following questions have situations or activities for which you should name persons who play an important role in your life right now. Kindly go through the questions and please enter their names. Kindly mention every name only once. These can be your friends, family, acquaintances, neighbors or your relatives in your home country or current country of residence or anywhere else in the world.

The following instructions were used in the online version. An instruction box named "How-to" will guide you further. So here we go!

How-to

• Kindly enter the names of the individuals one by one in the red box below.

• If you want to add more persons for the following situation/question, click "Add this person" so that the names are added to the blue box. You can add as many persons as you want (The blue box contains the names applicable for the question irrespective of whether the checkboxes are checked or not checked).

• You can use pseudonyms instead of the original name as long as you can remember who the real person behind the pseudonym is. So, feel free to write abbreviations or nicknames (For example: Raj for Rajee Kanagavel).

• If a situation/question doesn't apply to you, click on the "Next" button to go to the next question. You can also remove a person by clicking on the "Remove this person" button. This applies to all the questions in this section.

33. **With whom have you discussed personal matters in the last three months (for example, talking with someone when you were depressed, explaining your problems or expressing your happiness)?**

    The following "How-to" box was used in the online version.

    How-to

    • The names entered previously are shifted to grey box. The blue box contains the names applicable for the question. The named persons are selected by clicking on the check boxes and can be moved to the blue box using the arrows.

    • If you want to add new persons for the following situation/question, enter names in the red box and click "Add this person" so that the names are added to the blue box. You can add as many people as you want.

34. **Who are the people you have asked for practical help in the last three months (for instance, borrowing money or household items, or even asking them to help with small jobs like photocopying/taking care of the house when you were absent)?**
35. **Who are the people you have asked for advice in the last three months (for instance, asking for assistance in accessing information or asking their opinion regarding your stay or advice in making a difficult decision)?**
36. **Who are the people you have enjoyed socializing with (spending time chatting, playing games, going for a walk, watching a video/movie or even pursuing a hobby)?**
37. **Please list anyone who is especially close to you who you have not listed in one of the previous questions.**

Names	33. Discussed personal matters	34. Asked for practical help	35. Asked for advice	36. Enjoyed socializing	37 Anyone else?

In the following questions, I would like to ask for details of some of the persons you named in the list. If you had named more than eight persons, questions about randomly selected eight persons will be

	Name 1 ______	**Name 2** ______
Gender	❍ Male ❍ Female	❍ Male ❍ Female
How old is he/she?	_ _	_ _

What kind of relationship do you share with this person?(You can choose more than one option)	❑ Spouse/Partner ❑ Parent ❑ Child ❑ Sibling ❑ Colleague ❑ Cousin ❑ Relative ❑ Friend ❑ Neighbour ❑ Classmate ❑ Flatmate ❑ Other, please mention ________________	❑ Spouse/Partner ❑ Parent ❑ Child ❑ Sibling ❑ Colleague ❑ Cousin ❑ Relative ❑ Friend ❑ Neighbour ❑ Classmate ❑ Flatmate ❑ Other, please mention ________________

asked to keep the questionnaire short *(Online version)*.

How close do you feel associated/related with this person?	❍Very close ❍Close ❍Medium ❍Less close ❍Not close at all	❍Very close ❍Close ❍Medium ❍Less close ❍Not close at all
How long have you known this person?	❍Less than a year(Month(s)) _ _ ❍Year(s) _ _ ❍Since my birth	❍Less than a year(Month(s)) _ _ ❍Year(s) _ _ ❍Since my birth
How did you meet this person?	❍ Online ❍ Offline	❍ Online ❍ Offline
How do you contact this person and how often are you in contact with this person? -Face -to-face -Letters -Phone -SMS -E-mail -Instant messaging -Social Networking sites(Facebook, Google+,etc) -Other platforms(Skype)	Daily / Several times a week / About once a week / About once a month / Several times a year / Less than several times a year / Never ❍	Daily / Several times a week / About once a week / About once a month / Several times a year / Less than several times a year / Never ❍
Where does this person live now?	❍In another country, namely: ________________ In the country of residence ○ In the same state ○ In another state ○ In the same district/neighbourhood ○ In the same town/city ○ In the same house	❍ In another country, namely: ________________ In the country of residence ○ In the same state ○ In another state ○ In the same district/neighbourhood ○ In the same town/city ○ In the same house
How important is this person to you?	❍Very Important ❍Important ❍Moderately Important ❍Of Little Importance ❍Unimportant	❍Very Important ❍Important ❍Moderately Important ❍Of Little Importance ❍Unimportant
Now I would like to know how important y ou were in his/her life and whether you helped or provided support. Here are some activities/situations. *(You can check more than one option)*	❑Name 1 ..... discussed /shared personal matter with me ❑Name 1 ..... borrowed money from me or sought practical help from me ❑Name 1 ..... asked my opinion in making an important decision ❑Name 1 ..... socialized/spent leisure time with me	❑Name 2 ..... discussed /shared personal matter with me ❑Name 2 ..... borrowed money from me or sought practical h elp from me ❑Name 2 ..... asked my opinion in making an important decision ❑Name 2 ..... socialized/spent leisure time with me

	Name 3 ________	Name 4 ________
Gender	❍ Male ❍ Female	❍ Male ❍ Female
How old is he/she?	_ _	_ _
What kind of relationship do you share with this person?(You can choose more than one option)	❑ Spouse/Partner ❑ Parent ❑ Child ❑ Sibling ❑ Colleague ❑ Cousin ❑ Relative ❑ Friend ❑ Neighbour ❑ Classmate ❑ Flatmate ❑ Other, please mention ________	❑ Spouse/Partner ❑ Parent ❑ Child ❑ Sibling ❑ Colleague ❑ Cousin ❑ Relative ❑ Friend ❑ Neighbour ❑ Classmate ❑ Flatmate ❑ Other, please mention ________
How close do you feel associated/related with this person?	❍Very close ❍Close ❍Medium ❍Less close ❍Not close at all	❍Very close ❍Close ❍Medium ❍Less close ❍Not close at all
How long have you known this person?	❍Less than a year(Month(s)) _ _ ❍Year(s) _ _ ❍Since my birth	❍Less than a year(Month(s)) _ _ ❍Year(s) _ _ ❍Since my birth
How did you meet this person?	❍ Online ❍ Offline	❍ Online ❍ Offline
How do you contact this person and how often are you in contact with this person? -Face -to-face -Letters -Phone -SMS -E-mail -Instant messaging -Social Networking sites(Facebook, Google+,etc) -Other platforms(Skype)	Daily / Several times a week / About once a week / About once a month / Several times a year / Less than several times a year / Never ❍	Daily / Several times a week / About once a week / About once a month / Several times a year / Less than several times a year / Never ❍
Where does this person live now?	❍In another country, namely: ________ In the country of residence ○ In the same state ○ In another state ○ In the same district/neighbourhood ○ In the same town/city ○ In the same house	❍ In another country, namely: ________ In the country of residence ○ In the same state ○ In another state ○ In the same district/neighbourhood ○ In the same town/city ○ In the same house
How important is this person to you?	❍Very Important ❍Important ❍Moderately Important ❍Of Little Importance ❍Unimportant	❍Very Important ❍Important ❍Moderately Important ❍Of Little Importance ❍Unimportant
Now I would like to know how important you were in his/her life and whether you helped or provided support. Here are some activities/situations. *(You can check more than one option)*	❑Name 1 ..... discussed /shared personal matter with me ❑Name 1 ..... borrowed money from me or sought practical help from me ❑Name 1 ..... asked my opinion in making an important decision ❑Name 1 ..... socialized/spent leisure time with me	❑Name 2 ..... discussed /shared personal matter with me ❑Name 2 ..... borrowed money from me or sought practical help from me ❑Name 2 ..... asked my opinion in making an important decision ❑Name 2 ..... socialized/spent leisure time with me

	Name 5 ____________	Name 6 ____________
Gender	❍ Male ❍ Female	❍ Male ❍ Female
How old is he/she?	_ _	_ _
What kind of relationship do you share with this person?(You can choose more than one option)	❑ Spouse/Partner ❑ Parent ❑ Child ❑ Sibling ❑ Colleague ❑ Cousin ❑ Relative ❑ Friend ❑ Neighbour ❑ Classmate ❑ Flatmate ❑ Other, please mention ____________	❑ Spouse/Partner ❑ Parent ❑ Child ❑ Sibling ❑ Colleague ❑ Cousin ❑ Relative ❑ Friend ❑ Neighbour ❑ Classmate ❑ Flatmate ❑ Other, please mention ____________
How close do you feel associated/related with this person?	❍ Very close ❍ Close ❍ Medium ❍ Less close ❍ Not close at all	❍ Very close ❍ Close ❍ Medium ❍ Less close ❍ Not close at all
How long have you known this person?	❍ Less than a year(Month(s)) _ _ ❍ Year(s) _ _ ❍ Since my birth	❍ Less than a year(Month(s)) _ _ ❍ Year(s) _ _ ❍ Since my birth
How did you meet this person?	❍ Online ❍ Offline	❍ Online ❍ Offline
How do you contact this person and how often are you in contact with this person? -Face -to-face -Letters -Phone -SMS -E-mail -Instant messaging -Social Networking sites(Facebook, Google+,etc) -Other platforms(Skype)	Daily / Several times a week / About once a week / About once a month / Several times a year / Less than several times a year / Never ❍	Daily / Several times a week / About once a week / About once a month / Several times a year / Less than several times a year / Never ❍
Where does this person live now?	❍ In another country, namely: ____________ In the country of residence ○ In the same state ○ In another state ○ In the same district/neighbourhood ○ In the same town/city ○ In the same house	❍ In another country, namely: ____________ In the country of residence ○ In the same state ○ In another state ○ In the same district/neighbourhood ○ In the same town/city ○ In the same house
How important is this person to you?	❍Very Important ❍Important ❍Moderately Important ❍Of Little Importance ❍Unimportant	❍Very Important ❍Important ❍Moderately Important ❍Of Little Importance ❍Unimportant
Now I would like to know how important y ou were in his/her life and whether you helped or provided support. Here are some activities/situations. *(You can check more than one option)*	❑Name 1 ….. discussed /shared personal matter with me ❑Name 1 ….. borrowed money from me or sought practical help from me ❑Name 1 ….. asked my opinion in making an important decision ❑Name 1 ….. socialized/spent leisure time with me	❑Name 2 ….. discussed /shared personal matter with me ❑Name 2 ….. borrowed money from me or sought practical help from me ❑Name 2 ….. asked my opinion in making an important decision ❑Name 2 ….. social ized/spent leisure time with me

Now I would like to know how important you were in his/her life and whether you helped or provided support. Here are some activities/situations. *(You can check more than one option)*	❑Name 1 ….. discussed /shared personal matter with me ❑Name 1 ….. borrowed money from me or sought practical help from me ❑Name 1 ….. asked my opinion in making an important decision ❑Name 1 ….. socialized/spent leisure time with me	❑Name 2 ….. discussed /shared personal matter with me ❑Name 2 ….. borrowed money from me or sought practical help from me ❑Name 2 ….. asked my opinion in making an important decision ❑Name 2 ….. socialized/spent leisure time with me

Names of the persons	**Name 1**
	________

In the following question, I would like to know what kind of relationship one person in your network shares with another person, i.e., how well does one person know the other person? For example, how well does A knows B? Similarly, you have to answer for every other person you listed in the previous section.

Name 2 ______	o Intimates o Very well o Quite well o Acquaintances o Not at all	**Name 2** ______						
Name 3 ______	o Intimates o Very well o Quite well o Acquaintances o Not at all	o Intimates o Very well o Quite well o Acquaintances o Not at all	**Name 3** ______					
Name 4 ______	o Intimates o Very well o Quite well o Acquaintances o Not at all	o Intimates o Very well o Quite well o Acquaintances o Not at all	o Intimates o Very well o Quite well o Acquaintances o Not at all	**Name 4** ______				
Name 5 ______	o Intimates o Very well o Quite well o Acquaintances o Not at all	o Intimates o Very well o Quite well o Acquaintances o Not at all	o Intimates o Very well o Quite well o Acquaintances o Not at all	o Intimates o Very well o Quite well o Acquaintances o Not at all	**Name 5** ______			
Name 6 ______	o Intimates o Very well o Quite well o Acquaintances o Not at all	o Intimates o Very well o Quite well o Acquaintances o Not at all	o Intimates o Very well o Quite well o Acquaintances o Not at all	o Intimates o Very well o Quite well o Acquaintances o Not at all	o Intimates o Very well o Quite well o Acquaintances o Not at all	**Name 6** ______		
Name 7 ______	o Intimates o Very well o Quite well o Acquaintances o Not at all	o Intimates o Very well o Quite well o Acquaintances o Not at all	o Intimates o Very well o Quite well o Acquaintances o Not at all	o Intimates o Very well o Quite well o Acquaintances o Not at all	o Intimates o Very well o Quite well o Acquaintances o Not at all	o Intimates o Very well o Quite well o Acquaintances o Not at all	**Name 7** ______	
Name 8 ______	o Intimates o Very well o Quite well o Acquaintances o Not at all	o Intimates o Very well o Quite well o Acquaintances o Not at all	o Intimates o Very well o Quite well o Acquaintances o Not at all	o Intimates o Very well o Quite well o Acquaintances o Not at all	o Intimates o Very well o Quite well o Acquaintances o Not at all	o Intimates o Very well o Quite well o Acquaintances o Not at all	o Intimates o Very well o Quite well o Acquaintances o Not at all	**Name 8** ______

Next, I would like to ask few questions about you.

38. What is your gender?

- o Female
- o Male

39. What year were you born?

— — — —

40. What is your country of birth?

____

41. Do you consider your country of birth as your home country?

- o Yes
- o No

42.* Which country/countries would you consider as your home country/countries: (*Please name the country/countries).

____

***43.* Please provide the following details about the educational institution you are currently enrolled in.**

Level	Field	Which year did you start your current degree?	Which year do you expect to complete your current degree?
o Bachelor's o Master's o PhD/Doctoral student o Exchange/Guest o Other	____________	— — — —	— — — —

***44.* Please list chronologically all previous educational institutions you have attended in the past at university level or higher.**

Level	Field	Year of completion	Country
o Bachelor's o Master's o PhD/Doctoral student o Exchange/Guest o Other	____________	o Before 1990 o Between 1990 and 1995 o Between 1996 and 2000 o Between 2001 and 2005 o Between 2006 and 2010 o Between 2011 and 2013 o I have not finished yet o I was enrolled but did not complete it	____________
o Bachelor's o Master's o PhD/Doctoral student o Exchange/Guest o Other	____________	o Before 1990 o Between 1990 and 1995 o Between 1996 and 2000 o Between 2001 and 2005 o Between 2006 and 2010 o Between 2011 and 2013 o I have not finished yet o I was enrolled but did not complete it	____________

45. **Name two languages you speak and kindly rate your language skills**

____________ Basic – 1-2-3-4-5– Fluent
____________ Basic – 1-2-3-4-5– Fluent

46. **How well do you consider yourself to speak and understand the local language(s) of your current country of residence?**

- o Very well
- o Quite well
- o A little bit
- o Not at all

47. **How big is your city (currently living) in terms of its inhabitants?**

- o Less than 5,000 inhabitants
- o More than 5,000 but less than 20,000 inhabitants
- o More than 20,000 but less than 100,000 inhabitants
- o More than 100,000 but less than 500,000 inhabitants
- o More than 1,000,000 but less than 5,000,000 inhabitants
- o More t han 5,000,000 but less than 10,000,000 inhabitants
- o More than 10,000,000 inhabitants
- o I don't know

48. **How big is your University in terms of its students?**

- o Less than 5,000 students
- o More than 5,000 students but less than 10,000 students
- o More than 10,000 students but less than 30,000 students
- o More than 30,000 students but less than 50,000 students
- o More than 50,000 students
- o I don't know

49. **What is your current relationship status?**

- o Single
- o In a relationship
- o Married
- o Common law
- o Divorced
- o Widowed

50. **How do you pay for your studies and living expenses in your current country of residence? *(You may select more than one answer)***

- ☐ My family pays
- ☐ My own savings
- ☐ Part time job
- ☐ A loan from a financial institution
- ☐ Salaried position at the university
- ☐ Scholarship/grant/fellowship
- ☐ Other (please name) __________

51.* How did you find out about this survey? *Please select one option.

- o Personal email invite from Rajee
- o Facebook
- o University mail address invite
- o On the website of the research group
- o Salaried position at the university
- o Invite from another friend/colleague
- o Other (please name) __________

***52.* I'd be glad if you have any comments or feedback about the study**

____

____

____

____

Ta-da! You have reached the end of the questionnaire. Thanks a million for the effort you have taken to participate in the survey. I really appreciate your time and consideration. If you know more international students who would be willing to participate in this survey, you can forward the survey link. Thanks again. The summary of the results will be published at the end of the study on the website: www.transnationalsupport.de

If you have any question regarding the study or the questionnaire, feel free to contact me:
Rajee Kanagavel @ +49 5121 883 568, Email: kanagave@unihildesheim.de

Index[1]

[1] Note: Page numbers followed by 'n' refer to notes.

R. Kanagavel, *The Social Lives of Networked Students*,
https://doi.org/10.1007/978-3-319-96199-6

Printed by Printforce, the Netherlands